THE
WIDE
OPEN
SPACES OF
GOD

THE
WIDE OPEN
SPACES OF
GOD

A JOURNEY WITH GOD THROUGH
THE LANDSCAPES OF LIFE

BETH BOORAM

DIMENSIONS
FOR LIVING
NASHVILLE

THE WIDE OPEN SPACES OF GOD

A JOURNEY WITH GOD THROUGH THE LANDSCAPES OF LIFE

Copyright © 2007 by Beth Booram

This book is printed on acid-free paper.

Library of Congress Cataloging-in-Publication Data

Booram, Beth.
  The wide open spaces of God : a journey with God through the landscapes of life / Beth Booram.
    p. cm.
  ISBN 978-0-687-49096-7 (binding: pbk., adhesive, perfect : alk. paper)
  1. Spiritual life—Christianity.   2. Bible—Geography—Meditations.   I. Title.
  BV4501.3.B663 2007
  248.4—dc22

                                                                    2007006472

07 08 09 10 11 12 13 14 15 16—10 9 8 7 6 5 4 3 2 1
MANUFACTURED IN THE UNITED STATES OF AMERICA

To David, my fellow pilgrim

and the most beautiful human being I know

CONTENTS

ACKNOWLEDGMENTS

I AM GRATEFUL TO SO MANY WHO HAVE BEEN LOVING, caring, and supportive companions for me along this journey through God's wide open spaces. Here are a few I want to afford special thanks.

I want to thank Nancy Austel, whose vision inspired me to seek a publisher for *The Wide Open Spaces of God.*

I am indebted to the support of Ann Reynolds, Susan McWirter, and Dave Streit, along with Tabernacle Presbyterian's Women Alive, who opened their circle of friendship and launched me into the wide open spaces.

I am particularly grateful to my faithful team who rallied around me as we began the Wide Open Spaces retreat ministry: Mary Byers, Ros Carlson, Jan Daily, Lynn House, Sally John, Lisa Miller, Donna Rogula, Portland Schnitzius, and Pam Sechrist.

I want to extend a heartfelt thanks to a number of faithful and loving friends whose kindnesses have blessed me in significant ways over these last two years: Tim and Mary Byers, Pam Sechrist, Megan Foley, Roger and Judy Pope, Brian and Jan Daily, Sandee Falk, Brent Croxton, Portland and Todd Schnitzius, Janelle Puff, Linda Bannister, Zoe Croskey, and Vicky Didato.

Most of all, I am profoundly grateful to my family for their belief in me and their unwavering support: my husband, David, and our incredible kids, Brittany, Brandt, Brianna, and Brooke.

INTRODUCTION

The Wide Open Spaces of God

Submerged Dramas

THE DARKENING WATERS CLOSED IN AROUND ME; THEY felt ominous and suffocating. The diver in front of me continued to swim deeper and deeper into the ocean's depths. I knew that I was to follow, but everything in me wanted to turn back. My chest began to pound; my throat constricted. I've never had a panic attack, but I think this is what one would feel like.

A structure came into view on the ocean floor: a sunken ship? An open doorway led into a catacomb of hallways and complex passages. It was clear to me that the diver was going in and I was to follow him inside the belly of this cavernous shell.

Anxiously I turned away and looked over my right shoulder and above me. The waters were so beautiful, streaked with rays of light penetrating their expanse. I felt pulled toward them— toward the wide open, spacious sea.

Then it came to me. I had a choice to make. I could follow this diver and be trapped inside the sunken chamber and die. Or, I could turn out into the expansive waters of the ocean and live.

And then I woke up.

This is the kind of dream we don't soon forget. Dreams arrest our attention and awaken us to the submerged dramas brewing within us. This dream was so evocative, so penetrating, that I wrote it down because I knew there was something to it. I just didn't know what.

Six months later the meaning became clear. It was a Saturday evening, and my husband and I had been walking around all day like zombies, the magnitude of a decision we faced bearing down on our chests. We had been serving on the staff of a megachurch for several years. Through a number of devastating and disillusioning experiences, we faced the likelihood that we were going to resign from our roles.

In and out of process, we conversed with one another, considering our options. Finally, we concluded that there was only one thing for us to do: we both needed to resign. Once we decided, immediately we felt this amazing exhilaration—as if we had been set free and turned out into a larger, more spacious life. And then I remembered my dream.

It felt as if we were reenacting it. I immediately connected with the dream's images: the sense that I had a choice to make; the aversion of moving toward the complex, sunken structure; and the draw of the wide open spaces. The power of these images gave me courage. I sensed we were saying yes to life, yes to staying alive to our own souls.

I wonder if you have ever had a similar experience or sensation—a time when you knew that if you continued along a certain path, you would suffocate and die. And over your shoulder was a way that seemed right and that led to life, but it would take courage to turn that way.

The Wide Open Spaces of God

The wide open spaces is that view over our right shoulder. It is a time in our lives when God invites us to leave the life we have known—the comfortable, familiar, and established—for the uncharted, unfamiliar, and unknown wide open spaces of life with him. We yearn to move out into a bigger, more expansive, spacious life. But it always requires the risk of turning away from a smaller, more familiar, manageable life.

Many pilgrims of the Christian faith have hinted at these wide open spaces—the sense that God is much bigger and more gracious than we can ever conceive and is inviting us to live more freely and fully in his expansive presence. One such pilgrim is Eugene Peterson, a pastor, author, theologian, and unpretentious poet. I love the way he describes the wide open spaces in his translation of the Bible called *The Message:*

> Dear, dear Corinthians, I can't tell you how much I long for you to enter this wide-open, spacious life. We didn't fence you in. The smallness you feel comes from within you. Your lives aren't small, but you're living them in a small way. I'm speaking as plainly as I can and with great affection. Open up your lives. Live openly and expansively! (2 Corinthians 6:11-13)

Those Who Take the Risk

Living openly and expansively sounds good, doesn't it? Yet, oftentimes we find the reality of this journey somewhat vexing. Many of us seem to be hardwired with a strong nesting instinct, a preference for the predictable and safe, and a desire to remain in control of our lives. Consequently, we look at this *risky* expanding frontier with fear, caution, and ambivalence.

But when we are ready for this generous life, it is often because we sense our soul is shriveling. We are missing something, a bigger life that resonates more genuinely with our hearts. We've become tired or disillusioned and can't continue on the way we have been going anymore. The life we are living doesn't fit. And we know that we've got to make a change, or we will wither and die.

This phenomenon of a shriveling soul is an epidemic today. There are numerous factors that contribute to the soul's depletion: the pace of our lifestyles, our obsession with work, our compulsion toward busyness, and the neglect of solitude all ravage the soul of its energy for life.

In addition, people today are frequently in some form of crisis or another. Our marriages are strained, our children are struggling, and our finances are in upheaval. This kind of crisis takes its toll on us, especially if we do nothing to replenish and refurbish our soul. In the wide open spaces, there is potential for soul renewal that is integral to our health and wholeness.

We also venture toward this expansive journey as we better understand our unique calling. At different junctures along our journey, there are moments when we understand what it is that we have to offer the world: a beauty that we are to create, fight for, or champion.

My husband is a career counselor and is privy to this dynamic process that people enter when they begin to wrestle with their life's purpose. Often the individuals who come to him know that there is something absent from their lives. They may not know what it is, but their hearts are certain there is a life work they are better suited for than the one they are now experiencing.

To embrace and live out of our calling we often must leave the known and comfortable for the foreign and uncultivated. Blazing trails, we leave the recognized and begin to explore and discover the unrecognized potential within us. Like the frontier settlers in American history, we move westward because of some yearning we can't seem to quiet.

That same explorer spirit is awakened in those who become captured by the calling to expand their lives toward a greater good. My friend Megan, one of the most gifted young women I know, has been impassioned by a calling to serve impoverished youth in our city. It's as though she can't *not* listen to this burning in her soul and step out to care for the bigger world of poverty and injustice.

We also find our way into this expanding frontier when we catch a vision for a bigger life than the one we are living. Often, like Neo in the movie *The Matrix*, there is a "red pill moment" when our eyes are opened to a new reality that we hadn't seen as clearly before. We sensed that it existed, but we didn't know how to get there until the wool that had been pulled over our eyes was removed.

During this pivotal moment when the clouds part, or we sense God speaking, or we have an epiphany, we realize there is another way to do life that is better. We've been duped by our upbringing or the culture to embrace values that don't fit our hearts. And consequently, we have to differentiate and begin living by the values that really belong to us. God gives us a vision of living bigger, living a more grace-filled and robust life. So we set out with greater fervor, seeking him and the life he has for us.

The Bill Gates Story

Bill Gates stunned many of the world's onlookers when he announced that he would leave his role at Microsoft to focus his energies on leading the Bill and Melinda Gates Foundation. For three decades, Gates had been the CEO of Microsoft. His efforts had made him the wealthiest man on the planet—his net worth estimated at the time to be around $50 billion.

So what would inspire this shift in energy and focus? How is a man this committed able to turn over the reins of a company that he conceived and built up over the last thirty years? Gates said that his main motive was the desire to focus more energy on the issues that his foundation was taking on, issues of health and education in the poorest countries of the world.

Something about a greater good, a bigger story had captured the heart of the wealthiest man alive. Though Bill Gates has by no means lived a small, manageable life, he does seem to be responding to the yearning to live a larger, more altruistic life.

I saw news coverage of Bill and Melinda Gates, along with former president Bill Clinton, in Africa. They rambled among the poorest of the poor, observing a health clinic their foundation had begun. One would wonder how Bill Gates's old life behind a corporate desk looked to him, facing these uncharted, sprawling scenes of poverty.

Ambivalence

The truth is that most of us feel ambivalent toward these wide open spaces. There is something about the freedom and roominess that is alluring. Yet, at the same time, we are scared to death to leave what we know and head out on this voyage toward what feels like Neverland.

When I think of ambivalence, a poignant picture comes to mind. When our oldest daughter was two-and-a-half years old, her almost perfect world was disrupted by the addition of a baby brother. She would tool around the living room playing and then suddenly rush over to her brother, place her little hands on his tiny arm, grimace, and squeeze, saying "I looovvvvee yooouuu!" Her contorted expression said it all: "I love you *and* I want you to go back to where you came from!"

We have the same mixed feelings when we consider these attractive but intimidating wide open spaces. We love the thought of freedom, but we would just as soon go back to where we came from!

A Bigger God and a Bigger Life

The Wide Open Spaces of God is an invitation to open up our lives to a bigger God and a bigger life. It is a summons toward a more expansive life, one that is characterized by a keen awareness and responsiveness to God's presence and grace embedded in the terrain of our personal journey.

Through the varied terrain of life—its peaks and valleys, twists and turns—we have the opportunity to encounter God and discover who he created us to be. We learn that *all of life* is the context through which God shows up and reveals himself and transforms us through the very nature of life's contours.

David Benner, in his book *The Gift of Being Yourself,* echoes these thoughts:

> The omnipresent God whose name is Immanuel is not distant but nearer to us than we can imagine. God is not alien to the

circumstances of our lives but comes to us in them. Our challenge is to unmask the Divine in the natural and name the presence of God in our lives. (pp. 41-42)

God is not alien to the circumstances of our lives *but comes to us in them*. Whatever the landscape of your life, you can bet that God is in the center, inviting you to experience more of him and more of your true self through its topography. It can be challenging to unmask his presence. It requires practice, as we hone our spiritual sensitivities. But as we do, we will discover a growing, emerging life with God.

The Landscapes of Life

For years, I have thought and talked about my journey with God using the language of landscapes. Sometimes I would describe being in the desert, or the green pastures, or a valley of darkness. This language helped me frame the way life felt and describe what it was like to experience God in this new setting.

As I became more conscious of the landscape metaphor, I looked back over my journey and realized that it was composed of intervals that might be characterized as different landscapes. It was apparent to me that each landscape was unique, possessing its own distinctive terrain, and had an innate ability to transform my life, if I was open to it.

Even the more difficult passages had a strength and beauty of their own. I could see how each landscape had enlarged my life as I learned new ways of discovering God and myself through its contours.

Defining the Metaphor

As we journey into the wide open spaces of God, we will pass through a number of different landscapes. Though the types of landscapes are unlimited, this book will explore the terrain of eight distinct ones. Each chapter is devoted to a particular landscape, describing its geography and what we learn of ourselves and God as we travel through its environs.

Landscapes are not the same as a season of life. Seasons of life have to do with our age, changing roles, or stage of life. Landscapes are different; you can venture into any of these regardless of your age or where you are in your life stages.

These landscapes aren't in any sequence or order. In your own life, you can be in more than one landscape at a time. And you can return to any given landscape over and over again, spending any length of time while you are there.

Here's the key: no matter what the landscape of our lives, each possesses enormous potential to transform us, if we consent to be shaped by God through them.

The Reward of Doing Life "Right"

For years I worked really hard, trying to master the Christian life so that I could find my way to the "promised land" and live happily ever after. In my mind, that was the reward of doing life "right" as a Christian. Privately, I believed that there must be a magic formula or some spiritual secret I needed to learn in order to achieve this abundant life. But that secret kept eluding me.

Whenever I encountered a new landscape that didn't feel like the "promised land," I thought of it as a detour or an obstacle to get over in order to get back on track. Life always felt like it was somewhere "out there," just beyond my grasp. If I could only redouble my efforts, surely I would eventually take hold of it.

After years of trying to reach this land of promise, I began to wonder if my perceptions were skewed.

Life Is a Journey

About that time, my thinking started to shift. The spirit of God began to recondition me to understand life as a journey, not a trip to a destination. The goal was no longer finding my way to the promised land so that I could settle in and cultivate the best possible life for myself. Instead, the goal was to appreciate the journey, with the voyage itself becoming as important as the destination.

The second shift was understanding that life is not somewhere out there, but right here and now. If I want to experience a more meaningful life, it will be found by being present in the moment with God and living deeply in the landscape of life.

The wide open spaces of God include all the varied landscapes of our journey, through which God shows up, transforms us, and invites us to live a bigger, fuller life with him.

A Travel Guide

Many people I know don't have categories or language to think and talk about their journey with God. For most of us, life has been more confusing and disruptive than we had anticipated. Consider this book a travel guide, helping you name a few of the landscapes of your own journey with God.

Through using the landscape metaphor, this book will help you discover a way to frame your experience with God and talk about the different, surprising, confusing, or dissonant intervals of your journey with him. The result may be a more honest, adventurous, engaging, and intimate relationship, as you grow increasingly aware of God and yourself through the landscapes of life.

The Wide Open Spaces of God's Story

The Bible is full of courageous women and men who left the safety and security of the known for the unknown, uncharted, wide open spaces of God. Joshua and Caleb were among those whom Moses sent to spy out the rich and lush land that God had promised to Israel. They returned with a vision for taking possession of that palatial country. The other scouts, more content to remain where life felt safe, could only see the risks and obstacles involved.

A young maiden from Nazareth was visited by an angel and informed that she, an unwed virgin, would become pregnant with the offspring of God. Mary abandoned her comfortable plans to marry Joseph and *then* have children. Instead, she consented to let her small plans be disrupted, became pregnant out of wedlock, and endured shame from her community in order to become the mother of Jesus. "May it be to me as you have said," she replied, saying yes to God's invitation to a bigger, fuller, and riskier life (Luke 1:38).

Each of the landscapes we will consider gets its name from a biblical story. Some names are taken from actual places where the people of God traveled, like the desert or the promised land. Others are more symbolic names that describe the nature of the terrain, such as the valley of darkness or the green pastures.

Through the lens of each landscape, you will be invited to relate in powerful ways to these biblical stories and find great comfort in identifying with the characters. As you tour each landscape, you will learn to understand and interpret your own experience with God. You will be able to consider, study, or examine your own life story and discover God's involvement in the midst.

In each chapter you will read:
- A description of the landscape
- How we find our way into this landscape
- What we discover about ourselves in this landscape
- What we discover about God in this landscape
- What life skills we can learn by traveling through this particular terrain

The Past

The outcome of naming these landscapes is the ability to look back at our past to better understand some of the surprising, dissonant, or confusing intervals of where we've been. You will look in the rearview mirror at your life and see things you perhaps have never seen before.

The questions at the end of each chapter will invite you to stop, turn around, and look at where you have come from. You will have the chance to reframe your prior journey and, perhaps for the first time, recognize where God was at work.

The Present

This tour will help you not only look back but also live more consciously in the present. The only moment you can experience God is in the present moment. As you learn to be more attentive to life, you will become more aware of God and the bent of your own soul. You will start to notice God's subtle intrusion into the warp and woof of life. And you will be more conscious of your own heart, your deeper self that comes out through engaging with the landscapes of your life.

The dream that I described at the beginning of this introduction was meaningful because I was present to it. I could have remembered it and then never given it a second thought. But because I was present, I was aware of God revealing himself to me at that crossroads in my own life.

The Future

Finally, this tour will help you prepare for the future landscapes of your life with God. You will be encouraged to develop a realistic expectation of the journey ahead—for example, to give up expecting that if you do everything right, your efforts will buy a safe passage to some haven where you will live forever. When your life takes a turn toward some unfamiliar—even foreboding—terrain, you will be equipped with some life skills with which to navigate.

As you begin your journey through these landscapes, my prayer is that a spirit of exploration will be kindled within you, that your courage for adventure will be increased, and that, in the end, you will say yes to embarking on your own discovery of the wide open spaces of God.

A Sunset Epiphany

A few years ago, on a beautiful fall evening around six o'clock, I was driving back to work for a meeting. Heading north on a country road, my mind lost in some events of the day, I became aware of an obscured light over my left shoulder. About that time, I turned west and was instantly blinded by the source.

Before me blazed the most brilliant, startling sunset. The sun was a huge, fiery red ball—almost eerie in size. It overwhelmed the horizon and seemed as though I was going to drive right into it. Blushing pigments bled through the sky in either direction. It was such a dramatic sight; I think I gasped aloud.

Overcome by the landscape before me, my heart lifted in a moment of spontaneous worship. I lingered, my breath suspended. Then a thought entered my mind, like a whisper from God: "I'm bigger than *all* of this."

I can't begin to express the consolation I felt as I gathered those words to my breast and clutched them. At the time, my heart was throbbing with pain. I had recently been wounded by some personal attacks. The anguish I felt was intense.

God's whisper met me with profound comfort. He offered hope and perspective by placing my troubles in the larger context of his presence and purposes. God reminded me that he is bigger and more magnificent than anything I might face on this earth. Moreover, there was the confirmation of the whispered words in that beautiful sunset epiphany.

Over the next several months, I held on to those words. For a long time, I could return in my mind to the memory of that sunset and be soothed by God's whisper. Through this epiphany, I began to sense God inviting me to explore a bigger life with him, one that I now call "the wide open spaces of God."

There are times in our lives when we know we can't continue living in the same small, familiar, and cramped way. From deep within we feel the restless longing to move out toward a larger, more spacious landscape—one that doesn't constrict our soul and leave us for dead.

Then over our shoulder we spot a vista that catches us up short. It's so life-giving and inspiring that we are mesmerized by it. The sight fills us with breath and ignites our spirit, as we stand on the precipice.

Then it comes to us. We have a choice to make.

For Reflection and Conversation

• Using the language of geography, describe the landscape of your life right now.

• If you could physically visit any landscape right now, what landscape would you be most drawn toward? Describe it.

• At what time in your life have you been most confused, disrupted, or disillusioned about the landscape of life? Describe that time and why.

• Who are some characters from history, stories, or movies who left a smaller life to explore a more expansive frontier? What have you learned from them?

• In what ways, right now, is God inviting you to explore a bigger, fuller life with him?

THE
WIDE
OPEN
SPACES OF
GOD

- Chapter One -
THE DESERT

Exodus 13:17–17:7

A Gaping Hole

THE FIRST HOLIDAY AFTER MY DAD DIED WAS Thanksgiving. It had been three months since his death—not long enough to forget the horrific images of my dad's battle with cancer, but long enough to lessen the intensity of pain from losing him. Our caravan into the stark, brutal desert of death had lasted a year and a half. We watched Dad slowly waste away like the sandscape of a desert terrain eroded by the wind.

As usual, this Thanksgiving we all gathered at Mom's house, working together to prepare our feast. The kitchen brimmed with commotion, everyone scurrying around, darting between oncoming bowls of mashed potatoes and green beans, dressing and gravy, cranberries and sweet potatoes. We all tried to make this day seem normal, like it had always been. But I am sure none of us missed the barrenness of this holiday from the unmentioned, but felt, absence of my father.

Just minutes before we were to sit down, my mom, wrestling the bird, called out to anyone who might hear: "It's time for someone to carve the turkey." In that moment, a stinging silence filled the room. Each of us stopped, cringing as we felt the blow. A lump emerged from somewhere deep inside me and lodged in my throat. My eyes filled up with tears. My dad had always carved the turkey.

When we venture through the desert landscape and experience significant loss in our lives, we never know when we might bump up against a reminder of that loss. It can come out of nowhere. Unexpectedly, life reminds us that we are living in a climate of loss, living without someone or something that at some point meant everything to us. The presence of that person or thing is replaced by a gaping hole, a space that will never be filled.

The Landscape of the Desert

If you've spent any time in the landscape of the desert, then you know what I am talking about. The desert describes a time in life when we experience significant loss; a time when life is stripped down, dry and barren. The demands of this terrain require us to go without someone or something that, in the past, has been important and essential to us. We look around our life and notice the missing element, the familiar ingredient that mattered deeply but is no longer there.

In the arid desert, we feel the ache in our heart from our loss. We feel cut off from the lush life that was once ours and left in a place where so much tastes like sand in our mouths.

When we enter the landscape of the desert, we know the scenery has changed. Our surroundings look drab and dry; we have a hard time getting up in the morning to face another empty, monotonous day. Life seems bleak. And we have to keep living in spite of the fact that we have no energy left.

Entering the Desert

It's not difficult to think of ways we enter this desert terrain. It can happen when we experience the *loss of a loved one* through death, divorce, or separation. We lose someone so treasured that the landscape of life will never be the same. Every time we set the table or celebrate a holiday or pass by a room, we are reminded of their absence. A void exists where that person used to be.

We can enter the desert when we experience *the loss of belonging*. Have you ever experienced a move—a change in vocation or church or community—and your sense of belonging was disrupted and replaced by the feeling that your "roots were dangling"? We feel unattached, disconnected, and unknown. And we wonder if we will ever feel a sense of place again.

We can also venture into the desert through the *loss of significance*. For some women it can happen when they leave the workplace to stay home with a new baby. Though no doubt this baby is an unspeakable joy, the woman can still feel that she has lost connection to the bigger world and to herself. If leaving the workplace is often one bookend of the mothering experience, having children leave home can be the other. Many women find it difficult, after spending their best years mothering children, to watch those children leave and take claim to their own lives. The end result can be a loss of purpose and the lingering question of what to do with the rest of their lives.

For men and women, the experience of losing a job—perhaps being demoted or replaced by someone younger, more gifted, or more qualified—can be a devastating loss of significance. Somehow this experience taps into a secret place of vulnerability, where people question if they really have what it takes.

We can enter the desert when we experience a *loss of stability*: a job loss, financial loss, health loss, a loss of the known and the familiar. Life feels unstable, uncertain, and scary. I think of my friend Judy, a breast cancer survivor, who still shudders every time she walks back into the doctor's office for her annual recheck. And every time she experiences any health issue, her concern heightens because the "C word" still dangles over her life.

My Desert Wanderings

I entered my first desert landscape when my husband and I, with our four children ages six and under, moved from the small, rural college town where we had lived for seven years to a declining urban area north of Chicago. David was going to graduate school. For the first time in our ten years of marriage, our lives were separated vocationally. We had previously worked together in ministry on a college campus. Now I stayed at home with four small kids while he spent his days a half-hour away in seminary.

Everything about my life spoke of loss: I left many encouraging, loving relationships to move to a place where I knew no one. We had lived in a safe, homey, small town and moved to an unsafe, unfriendly, congested city. We left a satisfying, shared vocation and began a life where our worlds seemed only to meet on the floor of our living room, corralling four very young kids. We had enjoyed a comfortable and manageable lifestyle but were now under tremendous financial strain. I felt that I had left the green pastures of life for a stint in the barren, parched desert.

In fact, I began to refer to this time of my life as the desert. Desperately unhappy in this unfamiliar, unfriendly, and desolate place and overwhelmed with the task of caring for four small kids, I felt that my life was bleak and monotonous. It made me think of the forty years that the Israelites circled in the desert. I began to read their story and found myself relating all too much.

Israel in the Desert Landscape

I don't know if you are familiar with the story of the Israelites' wandering in the desert. While I spent three years in this landscape, they spent forty long and perplexing years there. The Israelites had gone to live in Egypt because of an unrelenting drought and ended up staying for 430 years. During that time, "the Israelites were fruitful and multiplied greatly and became exceedingly numerous, so that the land was filled with them" (Exodus 1:7).

The Pharaoh of Egypt began to fear the Israelites because there were so many of them. To protect himself from their dominance, he enslaved and subdued them through heavy labor. The Israelites cried out to God in their misery, and God responded by sending a man named Moses to lead them out of Egypt. Ten devastating plagues later, the Israelites left Egypt. They looked back over their shoulders to see the Egyptian army swallowed up in the Red Sea and moved forward into the desert, where they began a journey that lasted forty years.

The Long Way Around

I read the story of the Israelites one day during my trek in the desert and found myself riveted by this verse: "When Pharaoh let the people go, God did not lead them on the road through the Philistine country, *though that was shorter*" (Exodus 13:17, emphasis added). I was well aware of the impatience building in my own heart with my detour through this thirsty, colorless wasteland. As I considered these words, I got a sick feeling in my stomach that God was addressing me. It occurred to me that he was documenting my journey with a caption: "The long way around."

I hate the long way around, don't you? It's so inconvenient. Yet, it seems consistent with the way God works and his general practice in my life. Have you ever noticed that God rarely seems in a hurry? That he doesn't tend to take shortcuts? In my limited experience, I would say that has been the case.

Here's the rub: we live in a culture that applauds that which is faster. We are bred to be impatient, expecting things to move along like clockwork, demanding that life operate on our timetable. Anything that doesn't seem efficient or pragmatic is considered a waste of time.

God, however, doesn't seem to operate with that same economy of time. He doesn't seem interested in taking us the fastest way around. But he does appear to value taking us along a route that deepens our relationship with him and transforms us so that we become the people he created us to be.

The Desert Detour

That's not all that got my attention. God took the Israelites the long way around, we are told, because he didn't want them to face war and return to Egypt (Exodus 13:17). He knew that if the Israelites took the most direct path, the shortcut, that's what would happen. Israel wasn't prepared for war. But notice how the Israelites perceived themselves: "So God led the people around by the desert road toward the Red Sea. The Israelites went up out of Egypt *armed for battle*" (Exodus 13:18, emphasis added).

I don't want to make more of this description than it merits. It's hard to say what was in the Israelites' minds as they thought of themselves and what was ahead. They anticipated military engagement—that much is clear. And they must have thought themselves ready for it. Yet, God knew they weren't as ready as they thought they were.

This disparity offers an invitation to consider one of the most imposing obstacles to our spiritual life: our misperception of ourselves. God knew what Israel was ready for. He had an accurate appraisal of the Israelites' past experiences and skills, their strengths and weaknesses, and the landscape of their hearts. But they didn't seem to know themselves very well.

Sometimes we need a detour into the desert landscape because we don't know ourselves very well. I've become increasingly aware that what impedes my growth toward wholeness most is my own self-perception. I don't necessarily mean that I choose to deceive myself; I just don't always see myself as I am.

Until we take an honest look at ourselves and develop a more accurate perception, we won't be open for God to begin a transformational work in our hearts. We must see our need first before we are ready for God's reconstruction process to begin.

A Virtue of the Desert

One virtue of the desert is its ability to awaken us to the disparity between who we *think* we are and who we *really* are. When we experience loss, when life is pared down and the things we looked to in the past are no longer there to prop us up, we begin to see ourselves more honestly and become aware of what is in our hearts. The heat of the desert puts pressure on us, exposing our coping mechanisms. As it does, we notice our response to desert living and see some of the unhealthy ways we try to make life work for ourselves.

Like the Israelites' desert journey, our time in this terrain reveals things in us that we aren't aware are there. We start to see what we have ferociously clung to in order to give our lives worth and permanence: key relationships, material things, a certain lifestyle, or the feeling of importance from our position. And in the desert we, like the Israelites, discover things about ourselves.

What We Discover About Ourselves in This Landscape

We don't like to lose things. And often, when we do, our loss evokes a strong emotional reaction. That's what happened to the Israelites. From the start, the desert triggered a caustic emotional cycle in them. It went like this: they experienced loss that provoked anger that triggered blame.

They made it out of Egypt, passed miraculously through the Red Sea, saw the Egyptian army destroyed, and then three days later experienced loss: no water. They hit the panic button and became angry, grumbling against Moses (Exodus 15:22-25).

Now, I happen to feel that their panic was somewhat justified. After all, we can only live so long without water, let alone without water in a dry, arid desert. But it is curious that they didn't turn toward God to meet their needs after all that he had done for them. Instead, their loss provoked anger (grumbling) and instant blame directed toward Moses. And this wasn't the last time they would go through this cycle (Exodus 16:1-3, 17:1-3).

Have you ever heard that anger is a secondary emotion—that underneath anger you will find a deeper, more core emotion? If that is true, then what do you suppose was the core emotion beneath the Israelites' anger? In the next incident, we begin to see.

The next time, the Israelites complained about the rations. They were starving and looked wistfully back to Egypt where "we sat around pots of meat and ate all the food we wanted." Then the clincher: "but you have brought us out into this desert to starve this entire assembly to death" (Exodus 16:1-3).

In each instance, the Israelites complained that Moses led them out into the wilderness to die. It seems that what they feared most was being abandoned, being left alone to die. They were filled with terror that the very ones they hoped would save them would in reality desert them.

Abandonment is one of our primal fears. Think about a baby's separation anxiety. One of the first fears a baby exhibits is the fear of being left. As the Israelites experienced the real panic of not having what they needed to survive, that loss signaled to them that Moses and God were not coming through for them: those they had hoped would take care of them were, instead, leaving them.

Anger over Fear of Abandonment

When we enter the desert landscape through an experience of loss, we often find ourselves in this cycle of anger and blame. We process our loss as evidence that the ones who should be taking care of us, providing for us, watching out for us aren't. And if they aren't, there must be a reason. And the reason we fear most is that they are deserting us.

M. Craig Barnes, in his book *When God Interrupts*, suggests, "The deep fear lying behind every loss is that we have been abandoned by the God who should have saved us" (p. 123).

Have you ever felt abandoned by God? Have you ever felt that he left you alone in the wilderness of life? When God doesn't prevent loss or instantly replace what was lost with something even better, we often feel let down, forsaken in our hour of need. Anger and blame toward God rise up within us as we face the shock that he has abandoned us.

The Void Becomes an Opening for Intimate Companionship

He should have saved us. He isn't being the savior we thought he was. Our notions of God and the way he works are shaken up in the desert landscape. But if we are faithful and persistent, the void in our lives can provide an opening for him to become someone we may never have let him be: an intimate companion.

What relationship do you have that became intimate without the catalyst of raw, candid, honest engagement? Anger is our natural, normal, human response to losing something we hold near and dear. In the throes of anger, we wrestle with our companions and offer them our naked, hurting hearts. In the desert, when we experience loss that provokes anger and triggers blame, we are confronted with our aversion to expressing anger toward God: our honest, undone, hot anger.

In the dry, brittle terrain of the desert, when we writhe with pain because we have lost things that mattered deeply to us, I believe God invites us to come in brutal honesty and to offer him our anger over the way he is dealing with us. Only then can authentic, intimate companionship with God be forged.

In the movie *Forrest Gump*, a poignant portrayal of this strangely transforming exchange with God comes to mind. Lieutenant Dan—a volatile, bitter double amputee from the Vietnam War—clamors at the edge of his shrimp boat. There, with unbridled anger, Lieutenant Dan rages at God, lamenting the losses that have ravaged his life. In the next scene, we see him with a visibly altered countenance; it's as though the storm of his anger has subsided, and now the quiet waters of calm have taken over. By expressing anger, Lieutenant Dan made peace with himself and God.

The Cycle of My Emotions

During my time in the desert, I found myself overwhelmed with anger toward my husband. It was he who had brought me into this desert wasteland. It was he who was causing all this unhappiness in my life. And it was he who wasn't doing anything to make it better.

The experience reminded me of growing up. My older brothers would provoke me in some way, and I would come at them swinging. At that point, one of them would reach out his arm, place his hand on my head, and hold me at arm's length. I would kick and flail, my anger boiling over inside me.

I felt that David was doing the same thing by holding me at arm's length, keeping me at a safe distance so that he wouldn't have to take on my anger and blame. My feelings, though, were just a camouflage to hide my deeper fear—the fear of being all alone, emotionally abandoned, and forsaken by my husband. And by holding me at a distance, David was realizing my greatest fear.

The more I leveled anger and blame at him, the more resistant he became and the more firm he grew in his stance. His holding me at arms' length was a maneuver to duck responsibility for my pain. And honestly, he wasn't responsible. Certainly not entirely.

What I didn't realize at the time was that more relevant than my anger at David was my anger toward God. God saw through Israel's anger at Moses and recognized it as anger toward himself (Exodus 16:7). And the same was true for me. Ultimately I was angry with God, the one who I felt was dragging me unnecessarily through this godforsaken desert landscape.

Our Tendency to Blame

When we pass through the desert of loss, we see our tendency to look for people in our lives to blame for our misery, and we uncover our tendency to hold God responsible. We often blame him and others in an attempt to make them feel guilty or to feel pressure so that they commence the necessary efforts to rescue us.

If we can make them feel bad enough for our plight and convince them of how miserable we are, then maybe they will get on the stick and retrieve us from our desiccated desert. Our anger and blame *result* from believing we are being abandoned. We *use* our anger and blame to keep us from being abandoned.

Returning to Egypt

The terror evoked by the Israelites' fear of abandonment almost drove them to return to Egypt, a place where they at least experienced some measure of security. They preferred an abusive relationship of enslavement for the security of knowing where their next meal was coming from.

When we pass through the desert of loss, the pain can be so excruciating and the fear so overwhelming that everything in us wants to return to what we knew before. Even if we trusted in something unhealthy or harmful, even if we depended on it too much, the security it offered us was better than the vulnerability we now feel.

If you live with much self-awareness, then you probably know your "Egypt." You know the people, the places, and the things that you return to for security even though they aren't healthy for you. It is startling the lengths we go to, the price we pay, what we give up in order to feel secure and to avoid being abandoned.

As I languished in the desert, I found myself wanting so much to return to Egypt. I wanted to go back to my small, homey town where I was loved and appreciated. I wanted to go back to a meaningful life where David and I shared so much. I wanted to go back to a time when our marriage wasn't so hard, where we enjoyed each other and had fun together. But I couldn't go back.

Instead, I had to face the loss of so many things I had latched onto to keep myself afloat: my loving husband, life-giving relationships, a job that gave me perks, and a pleasant place to live.

Not that these were bad things at all, but I realize now that I had an unhealthy dependency on them. I needed them too much. I required them for my happiness. I locked onto them to keep me from feeling abandoned. But they were hazardous to trust in absolutely. They weren't enough to be my savior.

In particular, I had to begin to take an account of the demands I placed on my husband to be my savior. I realized that when I married I didn't lose my dependence on my dad to take care of me; I simply transferred it to my husband. I never really took responsibility for my own life. I never really grew up. I expected David to make me happy and keep me happy. And that was a responsibility he could not shoulder. Trying to carry that load for me would have crushed him. Demanding that he do it was crushing our marriage.

When we travel through the desert, we experience its climate. The landscape of our own desert is dry and desolate, a time of life when we encounter the loss of things that felt necessary to our lives. And we feel their absence. But in that precarious place of vulnerability, we open ourselves to God's becoming someone we never let him be for us before. Our loss creates space for God that had been occupied by other attachments. Against the backdrop of the desert, we begin to notice what we discover about God.

What We Discover About God in This Landscape

His Guiding Presence and Timely Provisions

In the Israelites' desert wandering, the strong feature they discovered about God was his unorthodox ways of taking care of them. He led them through a strange but visible representation of his guiding presence and cared for them through a peculiar but timely provision of food.

Each day God went before the Israelites in a pillar of cloud to guide them, and each night he went ahead of them in a pillar of fire to light their way. Neither the pillar of cloud nor the pillar of fire ever left Israel the entire time they wandered in the wilderness (Exodus 13:21-22).

This fledgling nation was returning to the land God promised them and learning to relate to God all over again. Just as parents walk beside toddlers who are taking their first steps, so God hovered over Israel, teaching his children to walk with him. God described his posture: "You yourselves have seen what I did to Egypt, and how I carried you on eagles' wings and brought you to myself" (Exodus 19:4).

That expression fits well the experience I had with God as I struggled along my desert path. I felt carried by him and drawn toward him, even as I winced with pain from all that I had lost in my life and marriage. Though I directed my conscious anger at David, my seething anger was really toward God, who had led me into the desert wilderness. My dialogue with God began to unravel. The parched atmosphere of the desert made me intensely thirsty for a more intimate and real engagement with God, and I began to seek him with earnestness.

What I remember most about his presence was a growing sense of acceptance and connection with him. Each morning I woke, slipped downstairs, made coffee, sat with him, and talked. The conversation became more candid; I started telling him what was in my heart, expressing my dismay at all the loss I was experiencing in my life. I began to seek him out of my intense thirst to understand him. I began to develop a greater awareness of his presence. I began to feel his acceptance of me in my raw condition and his encouragement for my longing to be authentic with him. I felt drawn closer to him, comforted by him, and full of desire for him. I felt alive to God, and he felt real to me.

When we enter the desert landscape of life, our spiritual thirst for God will likely be awakened with new intensity. We wrestle with who God has *not* been for us: a savior who protects us from losing things. And we wonder with greater curiosity about who he really is. As we give in to our thirst to know him, God's presence comes into focus and his companionship pulls us in. The psalmist describes the journey well:

Some wandered in desert wastelands,
　finding no way to a city where they could settle.
They were hungry and thirsty,
　and their lives ebbed away.
Then they cried out to the LORD in their trouble,
　and he delivered them from their distress.
· ·
Let them give thanks to the LORD for his unfailing
　love
　and his wonderful deeds for men,
for he satisfies the thirsty
　and fills the hungry with good things.
　　　　(Psalm 107:4-6, 8-9)

God cared for the Israelites not only through his strange yet visible guiding presence with them but also through the provision of daily food. Each morning they awoke to a peculiar meal: a fresh ground-covering of manna, a flaky substance that they kneaded into bread. And every evening, quail dropped to the ground around them and became their meat. They got water from rocks and saw bitter springs turned sweet (Exodus 16:11-15, 31). This was supernatural and happened daily—each and every day for forty years!

In my own desert, I had the opportunity to see God care for our needs with his own version of "manna." I think back to so many unusual and extravagant ways that he cared for us. Through an endowment of a person we didn't know, David's seminary expenses were paid for, books included. A couple of times I received cash in the mail from an anonymous giver. Perfect strangers sent checks to help us. I don't think any of those things have happened since. But they took place during my time in the desert.

I also look back and see that God taught us to live in the scaled-back landscape of the desert. We learned to enjoy some of the simple pleasures of life, the things in life that are free. We became avid patrons of the library and the beautiful parks that surrounded us. We enjoyed rich family time reading together, watching videos from the library, and playing games.

I learned to shop at thrift stores and look for bargains. We learned to share meals and be satisfied.

Sometimes I found myself resistant to cutting back, disliking that I had to say no to myself or take less than what I was used to. My pride said I deserved better. But afterward, I began to find these new practices soul-stretching. Having less, requiring less, demanding less cultivated a deeper contentment with what I had and a feeling of restfulness within myself.

Our journey through the desert expands our souls as we learn new ways of finding satisfaction. The topography of the desert enlarges our capacity for fulfillment in God and what he has in store for us. As we go without what we had and learn to receive what we are given, contentment finds its way into our souls.

Life Skills

People are not made to live in the desert. Its terrain isn't conducive to the survival of many life-forms. The following are some of the skills you will have the opportunity to learn as you live in this climate of loss.

Moving Beyond Blame to Responsibility

All of us have a tendency to blame those who appear to be responsible for the losses in our lives. When we blame, we fail to take responsibility for our own lives and the ways we need to grow up. Here are a few suggestions of how to move from blame to responsibility:

- Be honest with yourself and acknowledge who you are blaming and why.
- Write down all the ways you believe God or this person has let you down.
- Look over the list and ask yourself, "Are any of the demands that I have placed on God or this person unreasonable?" Mark the ones that you admit are unreasonable.

- Pray and offer forgiveness in your heart toward whomever you have blamed for your loss.
- Now, ask God to show you how to grow up and take responsibility for your life in the midst of loss; pray for his enabling.

Collecting Manna and Being Content

When we enter a time of life that feels desertlike, we learn to look for God's presence and the timely manna he provides. Each day, we are required to collect the manna that God supplies and learn to be content with what we have.

- Acknowledge your loss to God and ask him to provide for your needs related to this loss.
- Every day, look for small ways (manna) through which you receive what you need and give thanks for them.
- In the ways that you still feel empty, ask God to help you "befriend the emptiness" by going hungry and allowing the hunger to intensify your desire for him.
- Learn to accept and enjoy what you have and confess to yourself and God that "it is enough."

Experiencing Honest, Intimate Engagement with God

The pain of our loss can sometimes destroy our relationship with God. But it doesn't have to. It can become a catalyst for a deeper, more honest and intimate engagement with God. Here are some ways you can avoid letting the losses of life create a wedge in your relationship with God:

- Embrace the losses of life and grieve them.
- Abandon the habit of "dressing yourself up" for God and denying your anger toward him. (Your anger will come out one way or another, often in sarcasm or cynicism.)
- Learn to offer God your authentic self by sharing your unscripted anger and raw emotions. He can handle it!

The Desert Fathers

In the third and fourth centuries A.D., there was a growing movement of individuals who were seeking a more intimate, devoted life with Christ. They headed for the desert to discover that life. They gave away all their earthly belongings, kept only enough food for each day, and practiced a severe and disciplined life of loss in order to become more like Jesus, their savior. They lived out their intense devotion to Christlikeness in the desolation of the desert. These individuals are sometimes referred to in Christian history as our "desert fathers and mothers."

They chose the desert as a place of transformation. They identified the barrenness of the desert as a condition in which their hearts could become uncluttered and purified. They made the desert their home because they saw the virtue of its purifying asceticism, its cleansing starkness and simplicity.

Most likely, we will never choose the desert. But it will likely choose us. It is impossible to go through life without experiencing loss of some kind or another. The idea that God promises prosperity and that following Christ ensures that we never lose but only gain is simply not true. It's just not that way. Loss is a natural part of life. We can do nothing to prevent it. But there is a lot we can do to allow the losses in life to benefit us. If we will consent to let them create space in our life for God, then they will. And if we are willing to engage honestly with God in our anger and pain, he will become for us a real companion and savior.

For Reflection and Conversation

- As you consider your past journey with God, when have you spent time in the landscape of the desert? Describe what that was like for you.

- In what ways have you experienced loss recently? How has it affected you and your relationship with God? How has loss created more space for God in your life?

- Have you ever felt abandoned by God? What happened and how are you working through it?

- What is it like for you to talk honestly with God in your anger?

- How have you seen God's presence and provisions during times in the desert landscape?

~ Chapter Two ~

THE
PROMISED LAND

Deuteronomy 8

There's No Place like Home

LAST WEEK I SAW MY FIRST MONARCH BUTTERFLIES. THE
cadence of late spring has awakened them from their cocoons,
and they have begun to feed on the prolific milkweed throughout the fields of my geography.

Their recognizable black and orange wings were distinct
against the mild greens of springtime. I noticed one and then
another and then a dozen. Soon they were everywhere, flirting
with each blossom they greeted, and then catching a ride on
the winds of this open field called Hazel Dell Landing.

They were feeding, strengthening themselves, and storing up
for the journey they would make later in the summer. At some
point, each of these monarchs will begin a fall migration, a voyage that might extend more than two thousand miles. Their
destination will be a fifty-acre isolated region in the mountains
of Mexico. Obeying some internal instinct, their wispy bodies
will prepare for flight, following an encrypted map that leads
them to their winter home.

What is it in them that seems to direct their flight? What is it that, like a small homing device, tells them which way to go? Scientists can't explain it. It remains a mystery.

Monarch butterflies aren't the only species in the animal kingdom implanted with this internal radar. Penguins, homing pigeons, and lost dogs all seem to depend on this intuition. Invisible to the eye, these natural instincts lead them back home.

And what about humans? Do we have similar instincts, the same internal moorings which, if we listened more attentively, could direct us toward home?

In *The Wizard of Oz*, Dorothy seemed cognizant of her moorings at home. While she was in Oz, her persistent goal was to get back home. Finally, with Glinda's help, she clicked her ruby slippers together, repeated the mantra "There's no place like home," and magically woke up in her own bed in Kansas.

We know what Dorothy felt when she said those words. In our hearts, we long for home—to be at home. We long for the promised land.

A Literal Place and a Metaphor

In the Bible, the promised land is a literal place, a tract of land given by God to the nation of Israel. It is essentially the same land occupied by Israel today, though the borders have changed. The promised land also describes those times when the landscape of our life feels like home—as if we've found where we belong.

There are periods of time when we are more at home within ourselves, our world, and with God than at other times. During such periods, it feels as if we are living the life we were created to live. We're at home in our own skin, settled in the life we inhabit. One might describe it as living from our heart, from our truest self, living in our flow; and the result is a sense of fullness and peace.

A couple I know followed their dreams a few years after they graduated from college and married. He got a job in Colorado and so they moved westward, to the glorious Rocky Mountains, where they both enjoyed hiking, camping, and the great outdoors. Everything about their life felt good and wholesome, like it matched the deeper longings of their heart. Life was romantic, inspiring, and invigorating.

But after living for a few years so far away from family, they felt the draw to return to the Midwest, and they moved back. Though geographically they now live where they grew up, in many ways they feel as if they have left their homeland: a time and place when they were satisfied with a life that truly fit the contour of their own souls.

The sensation I am describing reminds me of a comment a colleague made to me. I had called to ask him to be a presenter at a leadership seminar I was offering. I left a lengthy message, describing the opportunity and what I wanted him to contribute. Not long after, he called back and told me that when he heard my message and listened to the invitation, it made his heart sing! That's what happens in the promised land, when we are at home in ourselves: it makes our hearts sing!

A Return to Eden and a Foretaste of Heaven

When we enter the landscape of the promised land, it stirs deep gladness in our hearts. Our passage through this landscape reminds us that we were created for home, that there is *no place like home*. I think our promised land experience in many ways is both a return to the Garden of Eden and a foretaste of heaven.

The idyllic setting of the Garden of Eden was brimming with everything Eve and Adam needed to cultivate their lives. More than prolific groves of fruit, Eden was the image of peace and wellness, growth and promise. When we experience a time of life when all is well inside and out, it is reminiscent of our roots, of the garden we were created to inhabit.

Not only that, when life affords us a period of promised-land dwelling, it is a foretaste of heaven. Something in us testifies that we were made for a different land, one in which our hearts experience deep peace and rest. When we diverge from the stresses and strains of life and linger in this landscape, our soul resonates within us that *this* is our natural habitat. We belong in this place.

A Season of Growth

We may inhabit the promised land any time we experience a season of growth in our personal lives, spiritual lives, relationships, or vocation. You might think of a time in your life when you were thriving spiritually. Maybe you were involved in a transforming spiritual community or reading a book that was really hitting home or experiencing a deepening prayer life. Whatever the catalyst, you were in a season of spiritual growth that made you feel alive and full.

One of my most memorable stints in this promising landscape was during the years when I was having babies. I loved being pregnant. Obviously, there were many challenges and lots of fatigue. But I was in my glory, overwhelmed with the miracle of giving birth.

There are times when we hit our sweet spot vocationally. A time might come to mind when your role fit you like a glove and you were living out of your calling. Your vocation seemed to flow from the essence of who you are. Parker Palmer, in his book *Let Your Life Speak*, describes what that is like: "Vocation does not come from a voice 'out there' calling me to become something I am not. It comes from a voice 'in here' calling me to be the person I was born to be, to fulfill the original selfhood given me at birth by God" (p. 10).

A Season of Peace

We may encounter the promised land any time we experience a season of peace, when life gives us a break from major conflict or upheaval. I've heard some parents say things like, "My family is at a really good place right now." I think what they mean is that everybody in their immediate circle seems to be faring well, and they are able to heave a sigh of relief.

I catch a glimpse of people enjoying these seasons when I watch an older couple stroll through a park, holding hands, content with each other and where they find themselves. Or when families ride by on a string of bikes, enjoying the peacefulness of a mild summer night. Watching a pontoon boat troll along, a retired man fishing off its rail, I sigh inside myself, sensing the deep satisfaction of his well-earned rest.

Season of Blessing

Anytime we experience a season of blessing we get a taste of this lush landscape. Life just seems to go better for us at certain times than at others. Have you ever noticed that adversity comes in clusters? In the same way, there are seasons when life seems to go our way, when we experience times of notable blessing from God. During these times, we absorb an unforgettable taste of deep joy. We have found our way home.

J. Phillip Newell, in his book *Promptings from Paradise* (p. ix), describes this longing for home as a longing for paradise. He suggests, "Although we may live in exile from the heart of life, promptings can still be heard from deep within us and among us."

Even when we feel far away from the promised land, there is a deep longing to find our way "home," to that place where we feel most ourselves, most in our element, living the life we were created to live. These promptings are a reminder of Dorothy's mantra: There's no place like home.

Israel in the Promised Land

When God called Abraham and Sarah to parent the nation of Israel, he promised them a very special land to inhabit. God said to them, "Leave your country, your people and your father's household and go to the land I will show you" (Genesis 12:1). Land, in Abraham and Sarah's day, was one of the most valued and significant assets in society. Nations were dependent on it for their livelihood and their identity. The better the land, the richer the natural resources, the more powerful and respected the nation.

And so Sarah and Abraham occupied this land promised to them by God. Their offspring multiplied, becoming the nation of Israel, until there was a terrible famine. During the famine they relocated to Egypt, where they remained for 430 years. Far from their promised land, the Israelites became slaves in Egypt until God delivered them through the leadership of Moses. They left Egypt and began a journey back toward home.

For Israel, the promised land was a literal place. For us, it represents those times when we get a foretaste of heaven on earth. But whether the promised land is a literal place or a metaphor, God warns us that this landscape comes with some handling instructions.

What We Discover About Ourselves in This Landscape

Over and over in Scripture, the promised land is described with rich language, espousing it as a fruitful, beautiful, veritable paradise. A fascinating comment is made of the land in Deuteronomy 11:11-12: "But the land you are crossing the Jordan to take possession of is a land of mountains and valleys that drinks rain from heaven. It is a land the Lord your God cares for; the eyes of the Lord your God are continually on it from the beginning of the year to its end."

Now, you would suppose that God cares for all the land on earth. But this comment seems to suggest that God had a special affection for *this* land—perhaps one of his favorite spots on earth—and it was this land that he offered to Israel.

What It Takes to Thrive

God gave the Israelites the very best land he had to offer so that they could flourish as a nation. He gave them everything they needed to thrive. "A land where bread will not be scarce and *you will lack nothing*" (Deuteronomy 8:9, emphasis added). And "when you have eaten and are *satisfied*, praise the LORD your God for the good land he has given you" (Deuteronomy 8:10, emphasis added). God's intent was for his people to thrive and be satisfied, to feel at home.

This tells us not only something of the heart of God for us but also something important about ourselves: we require certain conditions in order to thrive.

God loved his people and was attentive to their needs. He understood what conditions they required in order to blossom as a people. And so he called them to a homeland where all their needs would be met and they would prosper and experience deep satisfaction.

Do you know what you need to thrive? Human beings undoubtedly have some common needs that are essential for survival: food, water, shelter, and clothing. But each of us has unique needs and certain conditions that contribute to our well-being, conditions that comply with our disposition and constitution.

My garden has taught me something about this. My husband and I, over several years, have planted a host of perennials that return each spring and surprise us by the way they flourish.

Some of our plants have adapted well to our shady plot, while others clearly have not. As an amateur gardener, I am learning the needs of my plants and what it takes for them to thrive. And each summer, we transplant those that aren't flourishing to a new location where they have a better chance to make a go of it.

One of the virtues of spending time in the promised land is the opportunity to learn what you need as an individual in order to flourish. While living out of the deepest essence of your self, you can study the terrain of your life and determine the elements that help you blossom.

God has created us with common and unique needs. Our venture into this promising landscape acquaints us with those needs and the best conditions for meeting them. We learn how to cooperate with the bent and shape of our own soul and how to pursue, to the best of our ability, a life that honors our soul.

Misdirected Worship

As we discover a life that honors the shape of our soul and feel the immense pleasure of being satisfied with our life, we do run the risk of getting caught up with the "good life" and transferring our affections from God to it. That's what we observe with Israel—their bent toward worshiping their life in the promised land and forgetting God in the process.

A number of times, God warned the Israelites to be watchful over their hearts as they began to enjoy the goodness of life in the promised land. He said to be careful not to become proud and forget him once they began to enjoy all the blessings of the land (Deuteronomy 8:14). He warned them that they would have the tendency to attribute their wealth to their own strength and power (Deuteronomy 8:17). And he cautioned them that they might be inclined to think that God had brought them into the promised land because of something they had done to deserve it (Deuteronomy 9:4-5).

It is clear that God, knowing our hearts, warns us that when we experience this blessed life, our tendency is to worship *it* in place of him.

That is what happens, isn't it? When life is going well for us, when our horn of plenty is spilling over, we are prone to gather and hoard all the fruit. It feels as if we've hit the lottery. Before long, we become determined to do all we can to preserve the "good life" we are living.

Deep inside we might even fear that we had better hold on to it, because it's only a matter of time until it will be taken from us. Preserving it becomes the grid we use to evaluate many decisions we make: whether to upgrade our house, take the promotion, or stay home with a new baby. This life in the promised land becomes our paradise. And before we know it, we have sworn our allegiance to its conservation.

The promised land is a wonderful landscape that reminds us of how good it is to be at home. At the same time, it can be a treacherous landscape, because we often are smitten by its pleasures and form an attachment to it that looks an awful lot like worship.

What We Discover About God in This Landscape

God Makes Himself at Home

Not only did God bless Israel with an exceptional land, he also made them a promise that he would dwell with them in that land. What distinguished Israel from all the other nations on the earth was not that they had a nice home but that God himself made his home with them. When Israel left Egypt to go back to the promised land, Moses was given instructions to build a tabernacle where God would dwell. This portable home, more like a tent with movable pegs, enabled God to wander with Israel those forty long years in the desert.

Once they took possession of the promised land, this tabernacle came to rest, as did the presence of God in it. God explained, "They will know that I am the LORD their God, who brought them out of Egypt so that *I might dwell among them*" (Exodus 29:46, emphasis added). That is stunning! God wanted not only to provide a home for his people but also to *be at home* with his people.

We learn from our excursions in the promised land that God wants to live with us, dwell with us, tabernacle among us. He doesn't just give us a blessed life and watch from the sidelines while we enjoy it. Instead, he dwells in the midst of it with us, experiencing and enjoying the life we have together.

What this reveals of God's heart is remarkable: he yearns for close proximity and intimate relationship with us! That's what it means to be a family and live at home with one another. Perhaps one of the highest compliments you can pay someone is the desire to be with them. God's longing to be with us, to make his home with us, speaks of his regard for us—his desire to live with us.

This idea of God making himself at home with us is an image that surfaces throughout the Bible. Jesus used the language of home in John 15. He talked about us "abiding" in God and God in us. To abide is from the root word *abode*, a synonym for home. God wants us to be at home in him and him in us.

Jesus said that if we loved and obeyed him, then he and his Father would come and make their home with us (John 14:23). Paul called us a "temple" or home of the Holy Spirit (1 Corinthians 6:19). What an incredible thought—the Trinity making its home in us!

No other culture or world religion envisions a god who camps out with his people. More common is the view of gods who are far off, removed because of their austere otherness. Yet this God, the God portrayed in the Bible, the God of the Judeo-Christian story, is a god who comes near. He wants to dwell with his people and be at home with them.

Blessed to Be a Blessing

Not only does this landscape bring out God's desire to be at home with us, it also reveals his desire to bless us so that we can be a blessing. The Israelites struggled with turning God's blessings into the objects of their affection and an end in themselves. But that's not the way God intended it to be.

When God called Abraham and Sarah to this homeland, it was for the purpose of blessing them so that they could become a blessing to the nations.

> "I will make you into a great nation
> and I will bless you;
> . . . .
> and all peoples on earth
> will be blessed through you." (Genesis 12:2-3)

All along, God's intentions in providing this fruitful place of dwelling were so that Israel would be blessed and in turn bless *all* peoples on earth. He didn't provide them with these riches, this prosperity, this place called home so that they could enjoy it just for themselves. He intended for them to bless others from their own resources. He wanted Israel's light to shine brightly on the nations of the world so that others could find their way home!

In this land of promise, we are showered with the blessings of God and, as a result, are in a position to bless others. When we experience seasons of growth, seasons of peace, or seasons of blessings, we feel as if we have made it home. But it is so easy to stay home, to make our lives into a castle and live safely tucked inside, enjoying the comforts of home. However, God has something far more generous in mind for us. He has blessed us so that we can be a blessing.

The American Dream

I heard on the news recently that in the last twenty years or so, the average size of the American home has almost doubled. Yet, while home sizes have almost doubled, the average size of the American family has decreased.

At no other time in history has a culture worshiped their homes the way we do. I immediately think of all the home tours that have become popular these days. The last tour I took, I remember noticing the new trends of in-home theaters and spas. It seems that those who have the means are increasingly motivated to create a dwelling space that has everything, so there is no need to leave home.

Yet, here is an ironic statistic. Did you know that nowhere in the United States can someone working full-time at minimum wage afford a market-price one-bedroom apartment for their home? How can this be? This disparity tells us that we have forgotten we are blessed to be a blessing, that those who have are not sharing with those who have not.

So many problems in the world today could be diminished or eradicated if those who have so much would share with those who have so little. The problems of world hunger, contaminated water, and the spread of disease could be remedied if those who have would share a generous portion with those who are in need.

Undoubtedly God enjoys blessing people. It is obvious that he has a heart to give us what we need to prosper and flourish. But his intentions have always been for us to share the wealth, to offer some of what we have with those who have no place to call home.

Life Skills

Taking Possession of Your Life

There are three valuable life skills we learn along this path in the promised land. One of the most important is the skill of learning to "take possession" of the life God has given us. Numerous times God told the Israelites to take possession of the land he had given them. It's the idea of taking something that is given you and claiming it, or making it your own. Taking possession of your life is different from striving: it is not trying to get something that isn't yours, but taking hold of something that is.

- Take possession of your life by driving out your enemies. These enemies can be bad habits, compulsive behaviors, poor boundaries, shaming voices—anything that gets in the way of taking hold of the life God has created you to live.
- Determine what your enemies are and drive them out; command them to leave, refuse to entertain them!
- Take possession by claiming what is yours: the goodness of your life, your calling, your birthright as a child of God, and the gifts he has given you to enjoy and offer others.

Pursuing the Conditions That Help You Thrive

Another thing we learn about ourselves in the promised land is the conditions that help us thrive. Rarely do we have ideal conditions under which we live. And the truth is when conditions aren't ideal we learn to adapt, which actually produces deeper roots and stronger limbs. Yet, we are human and have unique needs that, when met, help us flourish.

- Pay attention to the conditions that help you thrive as a person and be at home in your own heart.
- Learn to create and pursue those conditions, in order to help you thrive and flourish. For example, if you discover that you function best when you have a creative outlet, then learn to seek ways to express your creativity.
- When you are not able to be at home in the most conducive environment, allow the less-than-perfect conditions of your life to teach you new skills of adapting.

Learning to Receive Good Gifts

And finally, in the promised land we learn to receive good gifts without making them our god. The world that God has created reverberates with so much goodness, beauty, and pleasure. And he has created us with capacity to enjoy it all! The literal promised land was brimming with abundant resources. And often our lives, when we stop to count our blessings, are equally full.

- God has created you with the boundless capacity to relish life's goodness. Learn to discover what brings you deep pleasure.
- God invites you to receive gifts and enjoy them with all your heart. But he warns you not to make what you enjoy into a god that you worship.
- When making an important decision, be careful to evaluate what will increase your spiritual, relational, and personal growth, not primarily what will increase your material wealth.

The Trip to Bountiful

In the 1985 film *The Trip to Bountiful*, Geraldine Page plays an elderly woman named Carrie Watts who has a physically weak but tenacious heart. She lives with her spineless son and conniving daughter-in-law in a small, stuffy apartment. Miserable and chafing, this elderly woman dreams of going back to where she grew up, connecting with a time when life was good and she felt at home.

Through dogged determination, Carrie sets off on a trip to Bountiful, the home of her childhood. Oddly, though the movie is not at all frightening, there is a continuous and prevailing suspense throughout. Knowing the frail condition of her heart, the viewer is left anxious and aware that she may never make it back home.

When she finally arrives, nothing, of course, is the same as when she left Bountiful. But it doesn't matter to Carrie. For her, the trip was a pilgrimage to try to piece together her past and her present, a trip to confirm the knowledge in her heart of a better place and time called home.

When she arrives at the homestead, weak and breathless, taking in the view of what was in her memory and comparing it with what is, she clutches the porch post. Welling up inside her is an evident satisfaction; the pied piper's song inside her has ceased. She is at peace now. She can rest now. She can die now. For she has come home.

A Place Called Home

If there is ever a time in life when we feel most at home, it is those times when God leads us to our Bountiful, our land of promise. Like Carrie or a monarch butterfly, sometimes we may need to travel hundreds of miles before we get there. Suspense may linger over us as we question whether our heart will make it and if we will have the stamina to complete the journey. But to our surprise, we discover a tenacity, a resolve that wells up from deep within. As we follow our hearts, we will find our way. Because our hearts know where home is. And there is no place like it.

For Reflection and Conversation

- Picture in your mind the one place in your world where you feel most at home. Describe that place.

- At what time in your life have you felt that you were living in the promised land? Describe that time.

- Right now, would you describe yourself more in a season of growth, peace, or blessing?

- What are the conditions most beneficial for you to thrive as a person? Describe them.

- In what ways does God want to be more at home in you? How might you invite him to be more at home?

- In what ways do you need to take possession of your promised land right now?

- Chapter Three -

THE MOUNTAIN
OF GOD

1 Kings 18:1–19:18

The Brawn of a Burning Question

WE WERE SO YOUNG AND NAIVE. HAVING ONLY BEEN married a couple of years and barely having cut our teeth as a married couple, we faced the unexpected: pregnancy. I was having symptoms that made me suspect that I was pregnant. But we were so inexperienced and unsure, we went to the library and peeked at books on reproduction in order to confirm our suspicion!

It took no time for us to embrace the idea of having a baby. So, I made a doctor's appointment and began the process of following what we hoped would be a healthy pregnancy and ultimately the birth of our first child. But from my initial visit, the doctor expressed concern. Then at fourteen weeks, after several doctor's appointments and ultrasounds, we were told that the pregnancy was no longer viable.

It was my first brush with personal loss and suffering, and I was absolutely devastated. I had given my life to Christ, committed my way to him, and trusted that he would protect me from pain.

For weeks I questioned God. How could he let something like this happen? What part did he play? Did he cause it or allow it? How could he be so cruel as to create life and then take it from us?

These unrelenting, unresolved questions were the impetus for my first trek up the mountain of God. Through them, I discovered the brawn of a burning question. From deep in the pit of my own grief, I shouted the questions that were burdening my heart. And they carried me up the side of the mountain, in search of a meeting with God.

Ascending the Mountain

We enter the landscape of the mountain of God through the portal of a burning question. Such questions often come at a time in our lives when we are experiencing some irreconcilable conflict, a dilemma we can't resolve, or an experience of disillusionment about our lives. Emotion building inside us, the only recourse we have is to begin a quest to get some answers to the problems that plague us. So, we set out on a journey, as if climbing up the steep incline of a mountain in order to seek an audience with God.

A variety of life experiences can instigate our climb. Sometimes it's tragedy that drives a person up the mountain. We can't get over what has happened—a loss we have experienced, a tragedy that seems inconceivable. Our innocence has been snuffed out by a punching blow, and we can't seem to take our next breath until we quiet a little of the pain that racks our lungs.

We know a couple whose world has been undone through losing a son to war. I received an e-mail from the father, peppered with questions of "what if?" Overwrought with the agonizing work of sorting through the debris of this loss, they are searching for some hint of resolution.

Another condition that goads us along this precipitous climb is prolonged suffering. Whenever we suffer unreasonably—when it is senseless and random—it seems our nature to ask God why.

People who experience unrelenting health issues such as recurring cancer, depression, chronic fatigue, or a string of hardships often are drawn toward this mountainous landscape.

Unanswered prayer can be a catalyst for many of us to begin our trek up the mountain of God. We pour our hearts out in prayer, asking for something we desperately desire, something that is good and noble, but we receive no response. The very thing we asked to happen doesn't, or the thing we asked *not* to happen does. God appears to be a "no-show," and the confusion and letdown incite us to begin a march upward, earnest to understand why.

At a pivotal point in one of our children's lives, she desperately cried out to God for help. From her perspective, God gave her a cold shoulder. His apparent unresponsiveness and indifference churned up a lot of questions and began a spiritual restlessness within her. She has been on a climb ever since, slowly winding along a jagged path, her spiritual questions pressing hard against her disillusioned heart.

At other times in our lives, we earnestly need direction. That need can also motivate us to move toward the mountain of God. We head up the steep incline for God's word to us, for clarity or wisdom. The decision we face seems far too risky to move ahead without assurance. And so we camp out on the summit, waiting for the answer we are seeking.

We can turn toward the mountain of God through a number of prompts: disillusionment, disappointment, fear, persecution, injustice, or spiritual thirst. What they all seem to have in common is the existence of a smoldering question and a commitment to seek an audience with God for an explanation. We become desperate to pursue God and gain a hearing with him.

Seeking the Counsel of God on a Mountain

Mountains are a favorite spot in the Bible where people met with God. Throughout the story of God, there are numerous examples of individuals who encountered God or sought the counsel of God on a mountain.

Moses met God through a burning bush and received the Ten Commandments on a mountain. The psalmists, Isaiah, Micah, and Zechariah all describe the mountain of God as a place where people come for a special meeting with God. Even Jesus journeyed up a mountain, where he met with his Father and was transformed by that encounter before some of his closest friends.

Elijah, an Old Testament prophet, had an unusual encounter with God on the top of a mountain. And it is his story that we will consider as we enter this landscape of the mountain of God.

Elijah was a prophet in Israel during the reign of King Ahab, a king with the dubious record of being the vilest king in all of Israel's history to that point. His wife, Jezebel, was equally treacherous, brutally slaying hundreds of God's prophets. Together, they flagrantly promoted the worship of Baal, a pagan god. As a result, the nation was a spiritual shambles.

An Event That Set Things Off

It's important to note that our journey up the mountain of God is almost always precipitated by an event that compels us to begin our quest up the mountain. We don't just happen into this space, unlike in other landscapes. We are driven there by an experience that ignites our spiritual quest to pursue God.

In the case of Elijah the prophet, he had forecast a severe famine in Israel. And, as predicted, there had been no rain, and a drought ensued for three years. At the end of the three years, Elijah summoned King Ahab, all the people throughout Israel, and all the prophets of Baal to gather at Mount Carmel for a showdown.

They met, and Elijah demoralized the prophets of Baal through a dramatic standoff. He had them build an altar to their god and call upon this god to set fire to the altar they had built. For hours, they shouted incantations and danced, but nothing happened.

Then Elijah called the people of Israel together, and "he

repaired the altar of the LORD, which was in ruins. Elijah took twelve stones, one for each of the tribes descended from Jacob, to whom the word of the LORD had come, saying, 'Your name shall be Israel.' With the stones he built an altar in the name of the LORD, and he dug a trench around it large enough to hold two seahs of seed" (1 Kings 18:30-32).

The story continues, describing how Elijah arranged the wood, placed the bull on the altar, and doused it with gallons and gallons of water. Finally, he called aloud to God and asked him to reveal himself to the people so that they would know that he was God and was turning their hearts back to him. "Then the fire of the LORD fell and burned up the sacrifice, the wood, the stones and the soil, and also licked up the water in the trench. When all the people saw this, they fell prostrate and cried, 'The LORD—he is God! The LORD—he is God!'" (1 Kings 18:38-39).

Backing Up Before Moving On

One day while rereading this story, I saw something I hadn't noticed before. After the prophets of Baal were deflated and it was Elijah's turn to build an altar, I noticed for the first time that he *repaired* the existing altar because it was in *ruins*. I imagined what it must have been like for the people of Israel to gather around the altar—to have to face its condition, a mirror of their own spiritual disrepair.

And then Elijah took the twelve stones, representing the twelve tribes of Israel, to rebuild the altar. He could have started over and built an altar from scratch, using all-new materials. But instead, Elijah used the rubble from the former altar, reminding the Israelites of their identity, where they had come from, and their history with God.

This incident spoke to me; it resonated with my heart and what I had been processing regarding my own history with God. I have noticed that when our lives are in ruins, we are tempted to look at the past and want to get rid of it all. We think we need to start over again and throw the baby out with the bath water. It's easy to assume that the rubble around our feet is of no value, that it is only the wreckage of what was.

Elijah's practice reminds us to gather what has been part of our story and has survived life's missteps, to treasure what is meaningful to our history and identity and bring it along in the rebuilding of our lives. It is often the way of God to make a colorful mosaic out of the muddle of life.

Moving On

Returning to the story, the moment Jezebel heard of what had transpired on Mount Carmel, she put a bounty on Elijah's head. When Elijah found out, he became afraid and ran for his life. That's when his journey began. That journey took him to Horeb, the mountain of God.

> And the word of the LORD came to him: "What are you doing here, Elijah?"
>
> He replied, "I have been very zealous for the LORD God Almighty. The Israelites have rejected your covenant, broken down your altars, and put your prophets to death with the sword. I am the only one left, and now they are trying to kill me too."
>
> The LORD said, "Go out and stand on the mountain in the presence of the LORD, for the LORD is about to pass by."
>
> Then a great and powerful wind tore the mountains apart and shattered the rocks before the LORD, but the LORD was not in the wind. After the wind, there was an earthquake, but the LORD was not in the earthquake. After the earthquake came a fire, but the LORD was not in the fire. And after the fire came a gentle whisper. When Elijah heard it, he pulled his cloak over his face and went out and stood at the mouth of the cave. (1 Kings 19:9-13)

What We Discover About Ourselves in This Landscape

If our journey up the mountain of God is prompted by a burning question, what do you suppose Elijah's questions to be?

If Elijah had any questions, they seem a bit veiled. When God asked why he had come, Elijah answered the question the same way twice: "I have been very zealous for the LORD God Almighty. The Israelites have rejected your covenant, broken down your altars, and put your prophets to death with the sword. I am the only one left, and now they are trying to kill me too" (1 Kings 19:10, 14).

At first glance, it might seem that he is simply making a report to God, as if telling something of which God isn't aware. Yet, there is a tension beneath his words that betrays his real questions: "God, are you going to let me be killed?" "I have been working really hard for you; are you going to take care of me?" "I am all alone; are you still here with me?" "God, will you prevail against our enemies?"

The Spiritual Energy of Authentic Questions

When we turn toward the mountain of God, the first thing we discover is the spiritual energy and earnestness that real, important, authentic questions unearth in us.

Sometimes, like Elijah, we may feel reticent to ask them, afraid that we might offend God or undo our faith. Maybe that's why Elijah was so indirect. Yet, God knows the real questions that pulse inside us, questions that uproot our faith and demand resolution.

Ken Gire wrote a beautiful and honest book called *The North Face of God*. Using the metaphor of climbing Mount Everest, Gire explains the north face to be the most severe and rugged face of a mountain to climb. His book considers the difficult and troublesome aspects of God that we will encounter on our journey with him.

In the book, Gire tells a story of Nobel prizewinner Elie Wiesel when he was a young Jewish boy and a conversation he had with his mentor, Moshe. Elie asked Moshe why he prayed. Moshe replied, "Man raises himself toward God by the questions he asks Him. I pray...that He will give me the strength to ask Him the right questions" (p. 11).

We raise ourselves toward God by the questions we ask him. Questions are good. Questions are fuel for our spiritual longings. Questions are what make us thirsty for God. When we ask the questions that life unearths, we become shot full of passion for our spiritual quest, an adventure that we might otherwise decline.

Why We Avoid Questions

However, too often we avoid questions. Trying to protect our faith from crumbling, we push away the questions we have about God. Unconsciously, we think that if we seriously entertain those questions, we will crack the door open to a weakening faith. Deep down we fear that we won't be able to find sufficient answers and that the result will be a splintering foundation that could lead to our spiritual ruin.

Another reason we may avoid honest questions is for fear that God will be angry if we question him. Perhaps we project upon God the response we received when we questioned an authority figure in the past. We feel sheepish, anxious not to offend God by daring to question his authority and involvement in our lives.

And sometimes we take on God's "public relations." We refuse to voice our questions because we are concerned about protecting his reputation in the world. We reason that if someone were to hear our uncertainty about God, they wouldn't take us *or* him seriously. (Could just the opposite be true?)

Do you know the real, authentic questions rumbling around in your heart and mind? Are they, as Moshe suggested, the right questions? Ones that will raise you toward God?

Seeking Security in the Answers

During these times when we are perplexed by the strangeness of life, our journey up the mountain of God acquaints us with our nature to question and our need for resolution. Not only that, we will likely make a second discovery: our bent toward wanting *answers* so that we feel more secure about our lives.

Elijah wanted to know if he was all alone, if he was going to be all right, if God had a plan. Why? Because if he knew the answer, then he would feel a whole lot better, a whole lot safer, and a little more in control.

We want answers so that we can predict the outcome of our situation. Answers provide information that help us know what is going on, what to expect, and how everything will turn out. If we have answers to our questions, then we can trust those answers, even if life still feels confusing.

We want answers because sometimes they are easier to trust than God. We like to have answers to our questions because sometimes they seem more concrete and substantial than God. Life has a way of disorienting us, and so we look for things that help us find our bearings. We turn, like a compass, to answers as explanations for our disturbance.

Have you ever noticed how hard people work to explain away pain? Our pat answers roll off our tongues as we try to feel better about the hardships of life. Are the answers untrue? Not necessarily. But they can also be a smoke screen we use to avoid acknowledging the confusing incongruities of life with God. We like pat answers because they seem more certain than a mysterious and sometimes elusive God.

God is not willing to be pinned down by pat answers or predictions. He is certainly faithful and consistent in nature. But he is not predictable and calculated. He is true to himself and always good. But he eludes being pegged by certain and confining definitions.

When we ascend the mountain of God, we often discover that we are more in search of certainty than we are in search of God. This awareness can become a catalyst for deeper engagement with God—a purifying and intensifying of our desires for him.

When we notice our obsession with certain answers and predictable outcomes, and wrestle with the reality that God rarely gives us either, we are at a defining crossroads. We will either dive into the mystery of who God is and decide to trust and enjoy him. Or we will continue to search feverishly for a religion that makes us feel that life is more certain than it really is.

Fortune Cookie Answers

I don't like uncertainty. And so many of the pilgrimages I have made up and down the mountain of God have been to bring closure to uncertainty in my life. Not long ago I was in such a place, wishing I had more details to fill in the blanks of my future.

One particular day I had lunch with my family at a Chinese restaurant. As is our custom, at the end of the meal, we ceremoniously read our fortune cookies to one another. When I opened mine I read, "You are headed in the right direction."

My heart leapt. "It must be a sign!" I'm sheepish to admit that at that point in my life, *any* answer, even from a random slip of paper in a stale fortune cookie, was a form of consolation to my unsettled soul!

A Universal Question

3| Finally, we make a third discovery about ourselves in this landscape. We discover the *real* question beneath our questions. Underneath many of the questions that propel us up the mountain are deeply personal and profound questions such as, "God, do you love me? Do you really care about me?"

Elijah knew God; he had an undeniable history with God; he had witnessed the dramatic power of God more than once in his lifetime. As much as he spent his life energies serving God, he was still asking a deeply personal and universal question of God: "God, do you love me; do you care?"

I tend to believe that the question of God's personal love is a universal question. In fact, I suspect that most people are deeply interested in the answer to that question. I also suspect that if we were convinced of God's personal love for us, few of us could resist it.

But we are not often conscious that we are asking this question. Why? Because it makes us so vulnerable. Recognizing that we are completely known by God, with all our dark shadows and shaming secrets, we find it hard to believe that God could really love us.

God is love. We know that. But we have doubts and difficulty believing that God has a personal love for us, that when he considers us he finds us lovable.

On the screen saver of our computer are dozens of pictures of our children from birth on up. One day I was passing by, dusting the living room, when an adorable picture of one of the kids popped up. From somewhere deep inside me gushed a blast of love for this child. I think it erupted out loud: "Oh, God, I love them so much!" Once the words were spoken, a very clear thought came to my mind: "That's how I feel about you."

I sat silenced, thinking to myself, "Could it be true?" Could it *really* be true that God loves me, feels the same way about me as I feel about my kids? The thought, I admit, was hard to take in.

Can you imagine when you float onto God's screen saver— when your face comes to his mind—that he has the same surge of emotion? Imagine God feeling a deep, personal love for you erupt inside himself. "Yes," he whispers, "I love *you* so much!"

This mountainous landscape invites us to embrace our questions—the incongruities of life that heckle us—and live out of our longing to know the personal love of God more deeply. During our journey, we are stretched toward God, invited to encounter his love and acceptance so that it is brought home to us. The mountain of God provides a climate for the love of God to transcend mere information and become deep heart-knowledge. Will you put the question to him?

What We Discover About God in This Landscape

When we arrive on the summit of God's mountain, often one of the first things we learn is how different God is than we had perceived him to be.

If anyone had encountered and observed Almighty God, it was Elijah. He participated in one of the most dramatic miracles in the Bible, one in which God, in no uncertain terms, declared his superior strength and power over all other gods.

And Elijah reminded God that he knew him to be a powerful God. The name Elijah used, *Yahweh*, speaks of God's immense and immeasurable power and autonomy. But was Elijah prepared for God to reveal himself in a dramatic way?

The God of Subtlety

Was Elijah prepared to encounter the God of *subtlety*? That's who he met. God instructed Elijah to stand on the mountain in his presence while he passed by. First came a powerful wind; next an earthquake; and finally fire. All three dramatic forces were recognizable ways that God had revealed himself in the past. Yet, God was not in any of them.

Then something odd, peculiar, and subtle happened: Elijah heard a gentle whisper. The word might suggest "the sound of gentle quietness or a gentle silence," as described in *The New Bible Commentary: Revised* (p. 345). I imagine it as the kind of sound you might hear walking in the woods when suddenly, for no known reason, the choruses of nature observe *Selah*—a rest, a hushed silence.

Interestingly, Elijah recognized God's presence in this peculiar stillness, pulled his cloak over his face, and went out and stood before God.

What do you suppose God was doing? Why did he appear in a gentle silence?

God wanted Elijah to know that he wasn't all brawn and bravado. He wanted Elijah to mature in his knowledge of God's subtleties. God turned before Elijah so that he could see a different facet of God's self, one that Elijah was not familiar with: the softer, more subtle side of his being.

When we make our way up the mountain, it is critical that we come with a willingness to allow God to redefine who we have known or thought him to be. The mountain of God is often a place where we experience a radical encounter with God, an encounter that can surprise us and invite us to view an unfamiliar expression of his manifold character and personality.

Scaling His North Face

I explained earlier that one of my first journeys up the mountain of God was after the experience of losing our first baby. I was dumbfounded, broken, and shocked that God, whom I had given my heart to, would permit such an awful, inexplicable thing to happen.

I cringed in pain, not only from the disappointment of losing a child we would have welcomed with open arms but also because I couldn't understand what part God had in such an experience. These churning questions propelled me forward in pain and anguish, desperate to understand and resolve my confusion. God invited me to scale his north face, the side of him that was hard to climb.

The outcome was a major shift in my knowing God more accurately and intimately. He tenderly met me in my story and his, helping me discover the constancy of his love and compassion. I grew to accept the reality that his love doesn't shield me from loss and hardship. I suffered disillusionment, wishing it otherwise. But in the end, I gained a greater respect and deeper experience of his true nature and compassion for me.

Our journey up the mountain of God is often a dramatic time of rediscovering who God is, encountering a facet of him that we had not known, or identifying ways that we have distorted who he is. During the climb, we often scale his north face and stumble upon the mystery and inscrutability of God's beautiful and true essence.

A Scenic View of the Unseen

One of the best parts of climbing a mountain is the scenic view you have when you reach the top. Climbing the mountain of God is no different. Here we discover a second virtue about God: his scenic view of the unseen reality.

Elijah complained to God that he, Elijah, was the only one left who had remained true to him. Elijah told God twice that he was all alone and that God's people were trying to kill him. But God gently revealed to him a different reality: "Yet I reserve seven thousand in Israel—all whose knees have not bowed down to Baal and all whose mouths have not kissed him" (1 Kings 19:18).

Elijah had been convinced that he was all alone, until God graciously parted the skies and let him in on a little secret: there were seven thousand in Israel who had remained true to their God.

Often we forget that there is more to be seen than meets the eye. We are so convinced that we know the whole story. But on God's mountain, he reminds us that he has a view of the unseen reality, a panorama of things that are hidden from our view.

Through our quest, we have the opportunity to enlarge our understanding of what is really true. It is a transforming experience as we get a fuller picture of what has been hidden from our view. And sometimes the pieces we are given fill in a hole that has plagued us for a very long time.

A Sign

In the novel *The Secret Life of Bees*, by Sue Monk Kidd, the main character, fourteen-year-old Lilly, had been plagued all her life by the haunting question of whether she was truly loved by her mother. Her mother's tragic death when Lilly was four had left Lilly adrift in an assortment of distorted memories and hurtful lies from her father.

Lilly was tormented by this unresolved question. In her private world, she would pray, over and over, for a sign that would settle this query once and for all and fill the gnawing hole she had for a mother's love.

One day, August, a woman who had known Lilly's mother, brought out a hatbox full of articles that had belonged to her. Settled in the bottom was a picture, the only one Lilly had ever seen, of Lilly and her mother. Suddenly, her eyes were opened to an unseen reality.

When she passed it to me, she held on to my hands for a second. The frame contained a picture of a woman in profile, her head bent toward a little girl who sat in a high chair with a smudge of baby food on the side of her mouth. The woman's hair curled in forty directions, beautiful, like it had just had its hundred strokes. She held a baby spoon in her right hand. Light glazed her face. The little girl wore a bib with a teddy bear on it. A sprig of hair on top of her head was tied with a bow. She lifted one hand toward the woman.

Me and my mother.

I didn't care about anything on this earth except the way her face was tipped toward mine, our noses just touching, how wide and gorgeous her smile was, like sparklers going off. She had fed me with a tiny spoon. She had rubbed her nose against mine and poured her light on my face....

I looked down at the picture, then closed my eyes. I figured May must've made it to heaven and explained to my mother about the sign I wanted. The one that would let me know I was loved. (pp. 275-76)

When we ascend the mountain of God, he often parts the clouds and graces us with a view showing a breadth and width of life that we didn't know existed. He may even give us a sign to let us know we are not alone, that in reality we are loved.

Life Skills

Just as if we were climbing a real mountain and would need to learn some skills of agility, endurance, and footing, when we climb the mountain of God we learn some wonderful life skills that will serve us well beyond the experience and into the other landscapes of our life.

Asking Good Questions

There is an art to asking questions, especially good ones. As we learn to live deeply with God in the midst of this landscape, one of the invaluable skills we develop is the art of asking good questions. Forming and articulating questions that flow naturally from our curiosity about our self, life, and God become second nature.

- Develop the art of asking not only good questions but also the "right" questions; ones that raise you toward God.
- Learn to live in the questions: *stay* with the questions that are propelling you upward and *wait* until you have the understanding you need to head back down the mountain.
- Practice the art of friendship. As you learn the art of asking questions, you will become a better friend to those in your life who need someone to draw them out and help them discern the questions that are stirring in their hearts.

Letting God Out of the Box

The second life skill we develop during our stint upward is letting God out of the box. We like answers to our questions because they are much easier to hang our hat on than a mysterious, sometimes elusive, and subtle God. What we have the opportunity to experience as we reach the summit of this landscape is a rediscovery of God, a redefinition of who he is or a glimpse of him that we have not seen before. But for that to happen, we have to let God out of the box we keep him in.

- Abandon the tendency to try to have God always make sense.
- Be honest about the stuff of life and of God that doesn't make sense, at least to us.
- Refuse to offer simplistic, pat answers to the complex and perplexing questions of life.
- Continuously rediscover and adjust your understanding of God.

Entering the Fray

This past winter I was watching a morning news show. One of the anchors was doing an interview with a family member of someone who had survived a plane crash. If I remember correctly, there had been eleven onboard the plane; nine passengers were killed and two miraculously lived through it.

As this news anchor engaged with a family member of one of the survivors, he asked a question that sent a chill down my spine: "So, do you think that someone from heaven was smiling down on your loved one?"

The question leveled me because of the implications of what he was suggesting.

What would he say next? Would he then turn to a family member of someone who died in the crash and ask, "So, do you think that someone from heaven was *frowning* on your loved one?"

That's what happens when we try to make life and God fit our own categories and boxes. Too often we settle for crude ways to make sense of God and life. And when we do, we come up with the wrong questions, like that one.

Incidents such as that plane crash invite us to enter the fray of life where God's story and our stories collide. From that collision, we can learn to form questions that raise us toward God, if we resist the seduction of simplistic ideas that keep God in a fickle, heartless, capricious box.

Will you enter the fray of your questions? Will you begin the arduous journey up the mountain of God, seeking an audience with him?

For Reflection and Conversation

- As you look back on your life, when have you ventured up the mountain of God? What were the questions propelling you? Describe that time.

- What questions are moving you toward the mountain of God right now?

- In what ways has God surprised you and shown you a different facet of who he is?

- What facets of God's "north face" do you find most difficult to understand and accept?

- In what ways is God inviting you to let him out of the box?

Chapter Four

THE VALLEY OF
DARKNESS

Job 1–2; 42:1-16

Afraid of the Dark

LYING STIFFLY IN MY BED, THE COVERS CLOSE AROUND my neck, I peered out into the darkness of my room. Shadows grimaced on the walls—cast by the moonlight streaking in through the windows. I noticed the door, closed to block out light from the hallway. It caught my attention as the wood grain swirled with ominous suggestions. The knotty holes formed eyes of monsters; the streaks of grain outlined willowy arms and bony fingers; the grotesque faces seemed to flicker with evil delight as they howled with open mouths in the darkness of my room.

That's how I remember it, lying in my bed as a little girl, paralyzed with fear of the dark. Do you remember being afraid of the dark? It is one of the most terrifying experiences of childhood, a fear that we don't necessarily grow out of as adults. Most of us have an innate aversion to dark places. We dislike the sensation of groping in the dark, unable to see where we are going and what lies ahead.

If you have ever spent any time in the valley of darkness, you understand the parallel. Traveling through this landscape feels as though a dark cloud has descended and is engulfing your life, obscuring your vision. Life feels heavy and hopeless, with no apparent source of light showing the way out. Immense sadness weighs you down from the fear of being enveloped by this dark embrace. Thwarted by your inability to see but not at liberty to sit and wait for the darkness to dissipate, you just keep walking.

When Darkness Descends

Most of the time when we walk through the valley of darkness, we know what has brought us there. One of the times it takes place is when we experience *deep turmoil in a significant relationship*—couples whose marriages are in an awful mess, and one they know they can't fix; parents whose estranged child has wandered further away from them and closer to the edge of disaster; individuals embroiled in a twisted and tangled conflict. There is nothing as traumatic as the collapse of vital relationships.

I also think of my good friends who have walked through years of darkness, taking blow after blow of *unexpected and unexplained difficulty*. They have lived in and out of darkness for some time, facing numerous health issues, a house fire, severe depression, an estranged teen, heartless betrayal, a devastating job loss. While others seem to enjoy prosperity, they have faced an unrelenting landscape of dark adversity.

Though most of the time we can point to the circumstances that lead to this time of darkness, sometimes it settles over us without warning or explanation. *We feel lost spiritually.* God seems far away, tucked back into the shadows of life. A sixteenth-century Spanish monk named St. John of the Cross wrote a treatise called *The Dark Night of the Soul.* I understand the title because I have spent time in that dark night. I know how disorienting the experience can be.

One of the most disconcerting summonses into the valley of darkness comes when *Satan himself delivers a pointed spiritual affront.* At certain times in our lives, we are keenly aware that there is an opposing, dark force pressing in on all sides, breathing down our necks. His intent is to wear us out through a perpetual onslaught of accusations and adversity and to intimidate us through the blackness of life's terrain. Exhausted and afraid, we fumble for an exit to get us out of this murky place.

One of the most common experiences of darkness for many is *depression*. Studies suggest that 30 percent of women are depressed and 15 percent of men, though those numbers are steadily on the increase (National Institute of Mental Health [NIMH], "The Numbers Count: Mental Illness in America," Science on Our Minds fact sheet series). Depression is a form of grieving—grieving the loss of something that we perceive to be critical to our well-being. In depression, we often grieve the loss of ourselves and the loss of hope that life will ever be good again. If you have struggled with depression, you are familiar with the terrain of this dark valley.

Whatever circumstances have led us into this dim tunnel, the challenge we face is that we have to continue living. We don't have the luxury of sitting and waiting for the darkness to subside. We have to keep walking, doing, and being while shrouded in darkness with no clear light showing us the way out. One of the authors of the book of Isaiah knew the sensation: "We look for light, but all is darkness; / for brightness, but we walk in deep shadows" (Isaiah 59:9).

My Own Journey into Darkness

For me, the valley of darkness came on the heels of the desert. After the desert, I thought for sure my husband and I were headed for greener pastures. David had finished graduate school and to our delight was offered a position in ministry where we had grown up and where our families lived. The longer I had lived away from them, the more I had begun to yearn for home. This seemed to be a clear indication that we were on our way to better days.

We moved from Illinois to Indiana in late October. It took a couple of months to settle into our new home and get our bearings. Thanksgiving and Christmas passed, and then one January morning I woke up depressed. I didn't want to get up. I didn't want to do anything. The day before me loomed gray and overwhelming. All I wanted to do was cry and sleep.

Over the next few months, I began to recognize what had been unearthed in me in the desert. Issues of unhealthy dependence, anger, and blame toward David were flushed out. I thought they would go away once we settled into a kinder landscape. Instead, they were brought to the surface and created a wedge in our marriage. I became overwhelmed by the darkness of depression, feeling trapped in a marriage to a man I believed didn't love me anymore. For the first time in my life, I understood why people divorced. The pain was so acute and intense, the chasm so deep and foreboding, that I couldn't imagine how we would ever recover.

I began groping about in the dark, unable to see which way to go or what was ahead. I cried to God in desperation, begging him to get me out of that black hole! But no light shone. Instead, my voice got lost in the dark recesses of life.

A Companion Named Job

If you are venturing through the landscape of the valley of darkness, then you will appreciate the companionship of Job. Some thirty-six times in the book of Job, the word *dark* or *darkness* is used to describe the horrific experience of this man. His lament is contained in these words from Job 17:11-15:

> My days have passed, my plans are shattered,
>   and so are the desires of my heart.
> These men [referring to three friends who came to visit] turn
>   night into day;
>   in the face of darkness they say, 'Light is near.'
> If the only home I hope for is the grave,
>   if I spread out my bed in the darkness
> . . . .
> where then is my hope?

The story of Job is a guided tour through this dark, foreboding land. It may be the oldest recorded book in the Bible and certainly is one of the most troubling ones. Job lost just about everything in his life because of a celestial clash between Satan and God, yet he is described as a man who was "blameless and upright; he feared God and shunned evil" (Job 1:1). The first scene in the drama takes place in God's heavenly palace, where the angels come to present themselves to God. Oddly, Satan comes with them.

> One day the angels came to present themselves before the LORD, and Satan also came with them. The LORD said to Satan, "Where have you come from?"
>
> Satan answered the LORD, "From roaming through the earth and going back and forth in it."
>
> Then the LORD said to Satan, "Have you considered my servant Job? There is no one on earth like him; he is blameless and upright, a man who fears God and shuns evil."
>
> "Does Job fear God for nothing?" Satan replied. "Have you not put a hedge around him and his household and everything he has? You have blessed the work of his hands, so that his flocks and herds are spread throughout the land. But stretch out your hand and strike everything he has, and he will surely curse you to your face."
>
> The LORD said to Satan, "Very well, then, everything he has is in your hands, but on the man himself do not lay a finger." (Job 1:6-12)

What is there to say when you read a story like this? If you are honest, you probably are thinking, "Now, that's bizarre!" Or, "Wait a minute. Do you mean to tell me that God suggested that Satan wipe out a man whom God called blameless and upright?" Stories like these are bothersome. They remind us that God is not quite as easily explained as we might think or prefer him to be.

So Satan went out from God's presence and began to wreak havoc. Systematically, he destroyed just about everything Job had; his livestock, his servants, and all ten of his children. And here is Job's response:

"Naked I came from my mother's womb,
and naked I will depart.
The LORD gave and the LORD has taken away;
may the name of the LORD be praised."

In all this, Job did not sin by charging God with wrongdoing. (Job 1:21-22)

Pretty remarkable, isn't it? I have to admit, his response puzzles me. I know I wouldn't react that way. I wouldn't exhibit that kind of acceptance after losing even one of my kids, let alone all of them. I can't imagine praising God after so much that I held precious had been taken away from me. And this isn't the end of Job's loss.

In chapter 2, Satan returns, this time asking permission to attack Job's physical body. Again, God gives him permission, the only caveat being that Satan must spare his life. What follows is Job's lament as he sits in ashes, boils covering his entire body, scraping them with shards of pottery and wrestling with God in the darkness.

The remainder of the book contains large sections devoted to the contributions of three pious and clueless friends who sit with Job in his misery. Finally, in chapter 38, God speaks up. Job is leveled by God's convincing self-disclosure and responds in repentance and worship. The story ends with this summary: "The LORD blessed the latter part of Job's life more than the first" (Job 42:12).

A Natural Aversion

In many ways, this story raises more questions than it provides answers. It feels risky to invite you into this story, knowing that you will feel a natural aversion to its awful turn of events. Nobody wants to be reminded that life can take a dark twist. If you are prospering, if life is pleasant and full, the last thing you want to hear is a haunting story that suggests life may not always be that way.

But those who are in or have been in the valley of darkness will probably feel some comfort. Just knowing that others have gone this way and survived is reassuring. Becoming aware that you are not alone, that others have traveled through the dark and come out on the other side, is consoling.

The reason I take the risk of describing this foreboding landscape is because I suspect that someday you will take a tour through it, and I want you to be prepared. I want you to know that it isn't abnormal for a Christian to travel through the valley of darkness. I want you to be ready for what it will bring out in you. And I want you to be ready to receive what it brings out in God.

I want you to know that you don't have to be afraid of the dark.

Two Parallels

Two parallels between our stories and Job's are valuable for us to consider. The first is an underlying cultural mind-set that was deflated through his story. People in Job's day had a particular worldview, one aspect of which was a belief in the law of retribution—the idea that people get what they deserve. They believed that people were rewarded by God for good deeds and punished by God for bad. Job's story confounds that notion because God himself said that Job was blameless and upright. Job's misfortune had nothing to do with any bad things he had done.

We have been influenced by this idea as well. Have you ever noticed that when you experience something bad, you sometimes wonder if God is punishing you for some hidden wrong? And when things go well, when your life is prospering, you take credit for being so good that God just couldn't help but reward you!

The second parallel is that, though the first two chapters provide readers with the story behind the story, Job never appears to have any idea of the celestial contest taking place between Satan and God. Not once is Satan even mentioned beyond the second chapter. Not once does Job seem to be aware that he got caught in the crossfire between God and his archenemy. Mike Mason, in his probing book *The Gospel According to Job*, has this to say:

> Surely this is one of the deepest enigmas in the story of Job—not just that such awesome power and privileges are bestowed with such seeming casualness upon this cosmic hooligan, but that the man who suffers so monstrously at Satan's hands is kept entirely in the dark as to the very existence of his spiritual foe. (p. 28)

Often when we pass through the valley of darkness we sense the presence of our spiritual foe. But though we may suspect his dark spirit opposing our lives, we never know the whole story. We know Satan exists; we just don't know all that he is up to.

What We Discover About Ourselves in This Landscape

Despair over the Loss of Control

As darkness descended on Job's life, what did he discover about himself? Almost immediately we see Job give expression to one of the most disturbing emotions one can ever experience: the feeling of despair. Listen to his words in Job 3:3-5:

> May the day of my birth perish,
>   and the night it was said, 'A boy is born!'
> That day—may it turn to darkness;
>   may God above not care about it;
>   may no light shine upon it.
> May darkness and deep shadow claim it once
>   more;
>   may a cloud settle over it;
>   may blackness overwhelm its light.

Job despaired of life and lamented that he had ever been born. That's pretty low. Have you ever been that low, felt so desperate, that you wished you had never been born? In Job's case, the cloud of darkness descended when he experienced a series of inexplicable losses involving his personal life. He lost just about everything. But his most profound loss was the loss of control. Job cried out:

> "What strength do I have, that I should still
>   hope?
> What prospects, that I should be patient?
> Do I have the strength of stone?
>   Is my flesh bronze?
> Do I have any power to help myself,
>   now that success has been driven from me?"
> (Job 6:11-13)

Job was helpless. And he was acutely aware that he had lost control.

In the valley of darkness, we are faced with our own helplessness and our inability to control our lives. We can't save ourselves. We can't find our way out. Again, hear the pointed words of Mike Mason:

> We Christians do not like to think about being absolutely helpless in the hands of our God. With all of our faith, and with all of His grace, we still prefer to maintain some semblance of control over our lives. When difficulties arise, we like to think that there are certain steps we can take, or attitudes we can adopt, to alleviate our anguish and be happy. Sometimes there are. But anyone who has truly suffered will know that when it comes to the real thing there is no help for it, no human help whatsoever. (*The Gospel According to Job*, p. ix)

One of the most unnerving aspects of my journey in this landscape was my recognition that I could not save myself. I could not rescue our marriage from the black abyss. I could not make things better no matter how hard I tried. I remember the panic I felt when I would cry out to God to patch things up but nothing happened. Losing control hit a raw nerve in me and sent shock waves through my entire being.

Our Commitment to Saving Ourselves

When we enter the valley of darkness, we face our revulsion at being helpless and out of control—and our defiant commitment to saving ourselves. Our quandary is described in the book of Isaiah:

> Let him who walks in the dark,
>   trust in the name of the LORD
>   and rely on his God.
> But now, all you who light fires
>   and provide yourselves with flaming torches,
> go, walk in the light of your fires
>   and of the torches you have set ablaze.
> This is what you shall receive from my hand:
>   You will lie down in torment. (Isaiah 50:10-11)

Lighting Our Own Torch

When darkness overshadows our lives and we begin to experience despair over our loss of control, we look for ways to light our own torch. Self-preservation surges within us. And we reach for anything that will offer us relief from our despair, relief from the agony of being helplessly lost in the dark night.

I understand the temptation to light my own torches. I know what it is like to look around for anything that will give me relief from my dark place of powerlessness. I think of others I know who have wrestled with the same temptation. I think of one dear friend.

Darkness descended on her life while she and her husband were living in a foreign country as part of a missionary team. It was an extremely trying time. Their belongings arrived six weeks after they arrived; their apartment was infested with mosquitoes; they had a gas leak; she was left alone most of the day with several small children; she felt alienated from the rest of the team, abandoned by her husband, and bored!

Oppressive darkness settled over her until, strangely, she began to feel some relief through a flirtatious relationship with a man she met. It started out innocently enough. But over time, this man offered her the affection and attention that she craved and that no one else was giving her. This illicit relief from the dark was too much to resist. She gave in to an emotional affair with him. Thankfully she was rescued before it became a full-blown affair. But she came dangerously close to the edge, close to lighting the torch of adultery.

When we enter the landscape of darkness and feel despair at our loss of control, we often face the temptation to light our own torches. Our survival instincts tell us to find a source of life that will stifle the pain or provide some semblance of light. Whether it's working harder, keeping busy, shopping, overeating, depending on alcohol, or having an affair—choose your own torch—each is an attempt to rescue our lives from the despair of darkness.

As you think about doing time in the darkness, what do you suppose your torch might be? Not that we can always redict how we might respond to the dark, but it can be helpful to anticipate our particular vulnerabilities. Like the bowl of ice cream I crave every night before I go to bed, each of us reaches for something to comfort us when the lights go out in our lives.

What We Discover About God in This Landscape

He's There and He's Listening

If you are willing to stick it out in the dark, you have the opportunity to discover what the darkness brings out in God. As we return to our story, we discover that God was with Job in the midst of the darkness, even though Job didn't see him. Job cried out,

> "How I long for the months gone by,
>   for the days when God watched over me,
> when his lamp shone upon my head
>   and by his light I walked through
> darkness!

Oh, for the days when I was in my prime,
when God's intimate friendship blessed
my house." (Job 29:2-4)

Job can't see God; in fact, we don't see God or hear from him until chapter 38! But when God does speak, it is apparent that he has been there all along. We can tell that he has been listening patiently as Job works through his grief, processing his sorrow with God as he mourns his losses.

God gave Job space to grieve and lament as Job tried to make sense of his life and remember who God was. Job's grieving process was formative, was essential to his being transformed in the valley of darkness. God's silence wasn't an indication of his absence but an indication of his posture of listening while Job unburdened his heart.

At the time, God's silence was agonizing to Job. And even knowing God was present didn't make Job's darkness any less dark. But God's presence did offer Job comfort, knowing he was not all alone in the dark.

God is with us in the darkness, even though we don't see him. His silence invites us to move into the pain in our own hearts. His silence causes us to ache for him, to call for him from a deeper place of hunger in our own souls.

God Is Leading Us Even When We Don't Know It

When God finally spoke, he spent four chapters reminding Job of who he was as the Creator in relationship to his creation. He didn't answer Job's question of why. He didn't explain all that had happened to Job. But he did turn Job toward what was real and undeniable: the constellation of stars in the sky, the vast animal kingdom, the weather patterns, and the varied terrain of the earth.

Why? What an odd response. Perhaps God chose to remind Job of the natural world because it was meaningful to Job, a sacred pathway toward God. Creation is one of the most important ways God speaks to me. Often when I connect with nature, something happens in my heart to refresh my memory of God's immenseness, his nearness and transcendence. It makes sense that during such a dark time of life God would point Job toward the concrete and tangible reminders of God's existence.

Whatever the reason, God spoke convincingly of his presence in the midst of the dark. And it worked! God was able to lead Job out of the darkness without Job's knowing he was being led. God did so by reminding Job that God was at the epicenter of the world surrounding Job's dark landscape.

That's the consolation we need as well. As we struggle through the valley of darkness, we often lose our sense of God's presence. We want to know that God is still at command central. We want him to lead us out of the darkness in ways that are apparent to us. What we often discover is God's cunning and craft at leading us out of the darkness *without us knowing* we are even being led.

Though all the reasons for Job's calamity aren't clear, it is clear that God wanted Job to know him more deeply, to know that he had not abandoned him in the dark. God issued a notice to Job that God hadn't been taken hostage by the darkness. God was still in control; he was bigger and more substantial than the darkness that permeated Job's life. All Job needed was a glimpse of God's eminence to make him collapse on his knees and repent of his doubts.

Then Job replied to the LORD:

> "I know that you can do all things;
> no plan of yours can be thwarted.
> You asked, 'Who is this that obscures my counsel
> without knowledge?'
> Surely I spoke of things I did not understand,
>   things too wonderful for me to know.
> "You said, 'Listen now, and I will speak;
> I will question you,
> and you shall answer me.'
> My ears had heard of you

but now my eyes have seen you.
Therefore I despise myself
and repent in dust and ashes." (Job 42:1-6)

God is with us in the darkness, even though we can't see him. And he can lead us out of the darkness without us knowing we are being led.

Circling in the Dark

As David and I muddled through the darkness in our marriage, I kept crying out to God to turn on the light. I looked for the magic formula, the right answer to get us out of our mess. We felt that we were just circling around and around in the dark. But in God's silence and our desperation something happened. We began to talk. We began to talk deeply and honestly. And for long periods of time.

We listened to each other and to each other's hearts. We rehashed all that we had been through and why it hurt so much. We revisited many painful memories that formed a wedge between us. Each of us was struggling to become more autonomous, to take responsibility for our own individual lives. Yet, we also began to fight harder for our solidarity and marriage as a couple.

Little did we know that God was with us in the midst of the darkness and that our "circling" was the process he would use to reconnect our hearts and heal our marriage. It wasn't a formula, it wasn't a strategy, and it wasn't an answer: it was the process of letting our hearts lead us toward each other, moving through the darkness together, that ultimately led us out into the light.

Our Darkness Is Light to God

In Psalm 139, the psalmist says to God:

> If I say, "Surely the darkness will hide me
> and the light become night around me,"

> even the darkness will not be dark to you;
> the night will shine like the day,
> for darkness is as light to you. (vv. 11-12)

The reassurance we have when we muddle through a dark day in our lives is that what is dark to us isn't dark at all to God. What obscures our vision has no impact on God's ability to see. In the darkness, you will discover that God is there, even if you can't see him, that he can lead you without your knowing you are being led. In this valley of darkness we learn that it is less important to see God and more important to know that he sees us!

That's why you don't have to be afraid of the dark.

Life Skills

Moving Toward the Darkness

As we walk through the valley of darkness, we can begin to develop some life skills. The first skill is counterintuitive. When we find ourselves in darkness, we need to move toward the darkness, not away from it. That is scary. Yet, if we are willing, we will discover unexpected treasures during our excursion through this grim valley. Listen to these words from the book of Isaiah:

> I will give you the treasures of darkness,
> riches stored in secret places,
> so that you may know that I am the LORD,
> the God of Israel, who summons you by name.
> (Isaiah 45:3)

Moving into the darkness is counterintuitive, like this tip from Senior Life Saving: If you dive in to save a victim, and in their thrashing about they get you in a headlock, move down into the deep water—*because the victim won't follow.*

- As long as you live in fear of the dark, it will keep you in a headlock.
- You must learn the counterintuitive skill of moving into

the darkness, not away from it; into the mess, the grief, and the pain of your life.

- As you do, trust God to lead you through it and out of it even without your knowing you are being led.
- As you journey into the darkness, glean all the treasures and riches that can be found in dark places.

Learning How to Grieve

The second skill we learn while traveling through the valley of darkness is the ability to grieve. Healthy grieving is critical to becoming a whole person. Grieving is the art of acknowledging honestly and accurately the pain in our hearts and letting God in as we do. Grieving is consenting to let life hurt us and admit to the pain.

- Process, embrace, and accept the pain, sadness, or despair you have experienced.
- Learn how to lament before God with all of it.
- Don't light your own torch!
- Instead, wait in the dark until the dawn comes.

Learning to Grieve with Others

If you learn to grieve well, you will also learn how to comfort others who are grieving in the valley of darkness. One thing that Job surely learned was what people don't need to hear when they are in the thick darkness of life. You will learn the same. By grieving, you will learn to grieve with others. And that is an invaluable lesson!

- Job reminds us that "men at ease have contempt for misfortune" (Job 12:5). It is easy to be like Job's friends— *until you become Job.*
- Remember what it has been like for you when you were in darkness; then offer that to your friends who are walking through this valley.
- Let them be where they are; don't hurry them along because their dark journey makes you anxious. Be

patient with the time it takes for them to find their way through the valley of darkness.

An Eclipse

A few years ago my family and I witnessed a lunar eclipse. We were driving back to Indianapolis from Nashville, Tennessee, where our oldest daughter attended college. We left at dusk, and as we headed north on the interstate, I noticed the moon overhead. It was a full moon but had a ragged edge on one side.

Over the five-hour trip we witnessed the moon's disappearance. Slowly the left side of the moon began to ebb away, diminishing with each hour that passed. By the time we were almost home, all we could see was a sliver; and then there was nothing. According to my sight, the moon had completely vanished.

Of course I knew better. I knew that we were going to have an eclipse, so I was watching for it. I even had a basic understanding of what happens during a lunar eclipse: the moon glides through the earth's shadow and for a short period of time is prevented from reflecting the sun's rays. And I knew it wouldn't last forever, that it was a temporary phenomenon. It all made sense, so I didn't panic as I watched the earth eclipse the moon, and the moon subsequently disappear.

However, when God is eclipsed by life's shadows, we don't have the data available to warn us. We don't have logical explanations for what is happening. And we don't know how long it is going to last. It feels as if we're watching a lunar eclipse: God slowly disappears, his presence obscured by the dark cloud that descends upon the landscape of our lives. Remembering that he is behind the cloud can be a tenuous endeavor.

Transformed Through the Landscape of Darkness

It is terrifying to experience the despair of losing control of our lives and the frenzy of being unable to rescue ourselves. Such experiences often unearth our long-standing dread of the dark.

But if you are willing to stay put in the dark, to still the impulse to light some handy torch and save yourself, then God will likely transform you through this valley of darkness. You will learn that when God becomes eclipsed by the darkness and you can't see him, he is still there. And whether you know it or not, he can lead you out of the darkness into the light.

For Reflection and Conversation

- Describe a time when you remember being afraid of the dark.

- Have you ever walked through this landscape of the valley of darkness? What was that like for you?

- What aspects of your life are you most afraid to lose control of?

- What are some ways you have learned to light your own torch to alleviate darkness in your life?

- What is it like for you to think about moving into the darkness in your life, rather than away from it? What do you fear most?

- What do you sense that God wants you to discover about him that will assist you as you navigate periods of darkness in your life?

- Who do you know right now who is in this landscape? How might you walk with them as a true friend during this time of darkness?

- Chapter Five -

THE GREEN
PASTURES

Ezekiel 34; Psalm 23; John 10:1-21

Burned Out

BURNOUT IS AN EXPRESSION WE USE TO DESCRIBE WHEN
we have gone beyond our limits or dishonored the shape of
our soul for so long that there is no spark left to keep us going.
We are dried up. The oil has run out. We are done.
And that is the very place Parker Palmer found himself.

After five years of conflict and competition, I burned out. I was
too thin-skinned to make a good community organizer—my
vocational reach had exceeded my grasp. I had been driven
more by the "oughts" of the urban crisis than by a sense of true
self. Lacking insight into my own limits and potentials, I had
allowed ego and ethics to lead me into a situation that my soul
could not abide.

I was disappointed in myself for not being tough enough to
take the flak, disappointed and ashamed. But as pilgrims must
discover if they are to complete their quest, we are led to truth
by our weaknesses as well as our strengths. (*Let Your Life Speak*,
p. 22)

Palmer, one of the outstanding educators of our time, left Washington D.C., where he had worked as a community organizer and professor at Georgetown University, and moved to Pendle Hill, a Quaker living-and-learning community, where he spent the next eleven years rediscovering himself and his vocational calling.

His sabbatical at Pendle Hill was the very assignment he needed to be restored in his soul and awakened to his own destiny. Palmer wrote, "I have become clear about at least one thing: self-care is never a selfish act—it is simply good stewardship of the only gift I have, the gift I was put on earth to offer to others" (p. 30).

There are times in our lives when we feel that we have burned out. Our weaknesses have led us to the truth that we can't keep living the way we've been living. Exhausted by the frenetic pace of life's treadmill, worn out by all the demands that press in on us, drained by years of continuing to give without being refilled, our soul cries for a respite. We look for someplace we can hide out and get away from it all, some hidden-away room in life where we can sneak off and not be found.

What we may not know is that we long for the landscape of green pastures: a place we are drawn toward by God for the renewal of our souls. In this peaceful and restful landscape, we find nourishment, regain our bearings, and are healed from the maladies of life. Our shepherd God chooses this grazing pasture to restore our weary souls.

Visit to a Spa

If we were to compare this landscape to something in our everyday lives, it might be a spa. Whether you've ever visited a spa or not, you may know that its purpose is to provide special services that fill you back up after becoming depleted; it rejuvenates, restores, and refreshes you back to health. That's what we encounter when we recuperate in the landscape of green pastures.

This landscape is of essential importance to us, yet probably the one least visited. Why? Because we have to choose to go there.

Many of the landscapes we journey through in life we do not choose. No one chooses to enter the valley of darkness or the landscape of exile. But this landscape is different. Rarely will life lead us to this place of rest and quiet. However, we will frequently be invited there by our shepherd. We must learn to accept the invitation!

Our Ticket to Greener Pastures

A number of life situations may create our need to graze in green pastures.

Sometimes we need the green pastures because we've given too much! Those who are primary caregivers to others, especially highly needy or dependent others, often get worn out through the unending demands placed on them. Parents of young children, teachers, nurses, doctors, counselors, single parents, and families caring for the sick or elderly are some who qualify for entrance into these verdant pastures.

Sometimes we need the green pastures because we've lost our moorings. During transitional times of life, it's not uncommon to become disoriented about who we are. Those "between times" can leave us confused about our identity: who we are, what we want, what we have to offer, what matters to us. The green pastures are a wonderful place to become reconnected with our own desires, preferences, passions, and dreams.

Sometimes we need the green pastures because we've been beaten up by life. People with broken hearts will find comfort in this restoring respite. Those who have suffered the loss of relationship, experienced betrayal, been devastated by tragedy, suffered from chronic pain—physically, emotionally, mentally, or spiritually—are people who need a holiday in this lush pastureland of God.

Life creates a need for the green pastures, and God is delighted to lead us toward them. But we don't just end up there; we must choose to go.

A Portrait of God

The One who beckons us toward this place of rest and healing is described as a shepherd, an image of God portrayed throughout the Bible. Oddly enough, in biblical times the vocation of shepherding wasn't an esteemed career. It was considered a loathsome vocation. Yet again and again in the Bible, God is identified as a shepherd!

The first reference to God as a shepherd appears in Genesis 48, when Jacob is blessing Joseph's sons and refers to him as "the God who has been my shepherd / all my life to this day" (v. 15). The image surfaces in the writings of David and the psalmists, most of the major and minor prophets, and the words of the gospel writers. In fact, Jesus referred to himself as a shepherd.

In the book of Revelation, John sees a vision of all the people who have survived the tribulation gathering around the throne of Christ, and one of the elders at the throne says:

> He who sits on the throne will spread his tent over
> them.
> Never again will they hunger;
> never again will they thirst.
> The sun will not beat upon them,
> nor any scorching heat.
> For the Lamb at the center of the throne will be their
> shepherd;
> he will lead them to springs of living
> water.
> And God will wipe away every tear from their eyes.
> (Revelation 7:15-17)

The Bible is full of descriptive detail that paints a portrait of God as our shepherd and us as his sheep. I want to focus on three distinct images within that portrait: a shepherd who leads his sheep to pasture; a shepherd who rescues his lost sheep; and a shepherdess who heals her hurting sheep. As we consider each image, *I will combine what we discover about ourselves with what we discover about God in this landscape.*

The First Image: A Shepherd Who Leads His Sheep to Pasture

Picture a shepherd with a ruddy complexion and tough-soled feet, padding down a rocky path with a sheep nestled around his neck. Imagine his large hands clasping the feet gently but firmly as he nestles his head toward the sheep's face. The sheep responds, turning its face toward the shepherd's with a look of simple trust and relief, as it is carried back to safe pasture. Take a moment and meditate on this image in your mind.

What We Discover About Ourselves in This Landscape

Our Resistance to Rest

The landscape of the green pastures is a time in life when God wants us to slow down and rest. But when we enter this landscape we discover what it brings out in us: our *resistance to rest.* "The LORD is my shepherd, I shall not be in want. / He *makes* me lie down in green pastures" (Psalm 23:1-2, emphasis added). David seems quite intentional when he describes God's shepherding in this way. David wasn't one to lie down on his own. He wasn't one to rest on his own. And neither are we.

The same idea is expressed in Ezekiel 34:15, when God says, "I myself will tend my sheep and *have them lie down*" (emphasis added). Both these verses seem to suggest that we don't lie down on our own: we often need to be coaxed or coerced.

When we are in need of rest because we are worn out from the stresses of life, God invites us to take time in the green pastures. But more than likely we will need some help lying down.

Help Lying Down

One of the most stressful times of my life was during the weeks leading to my father's death from cancer. My brothers and I would take turns spending the night to help take care of Dad. I was exhausted, depleted, and running on adrenaline.

One morning, while in too much of a hurry, I went bounding down the stairs, missed a few steps, and broke my foot. I had never broken a bone in my life. And there I was, incapacitated, at such a stressful time!

For days, all I could do was sit on my back deck with my foot elevated in an ice boot. As I did, I read, prayed, journaled, and reflected on the journey I was on. It wasn't a respite I would have chosen. In fact, at first I deeply resented it. But over time, as I gave in to it, I began to feel myself filling up. My heart was replenished with rest and calmness.

I would never have chosen to lie down, but when I was forced to, not only did my foot begin to heal, my soul was restored. And I drew from that reserve as I pressed through the valley of my father's death.

Why It's Hard to Rest

Why do we find it so difficult to rest? Why do we often need to experience a *forced* Sabbath? Here are some possibilities:

We feel frustrated that we have limits and tend to neglect them. Our culture presses us to overextend ourselves. Most advances in technology are advances that extend us beyond our limits: cell phones, computers, pagers, electronic organizers. Something's always beeping! We are pressured always to be "on call" and feel selfish if we aren't.

We feel weak or selfish if we take care of ourselves. We reason that we don't deserve to be gentle with ourselves—that's for wimps. It's often perceived as a badge of honor to be exhausted and overextended rather than to live with a more reasonable rhythm to life and to take care of ourselves.

We feel internal resistance or discomfort when we rest, and so we avoid whatever causes this internal conflict. We have been led to believe, "If I am doing things right, then it will feel right." Resting doesn't often feel right—at first. We have to confront the resistance within us and press through it before we can glean the benefits of rest.

What We Discover About God in This Landscape

The LORD is my shepherd, I shall not be in want.
He makes me lie down in green pastures,
he leads me beside quiet waters,
he restores my soul.

The Twenty-third Psalm is the best-known and perhaps the most poignant passage describing God as our shepherd who leads us toward green pastures where we can rest, be nourished, and be restored.

Jesus adds detail to the portrait of our pastoring shepherd. He says that he calls each one of us *by name* as he leads us toward safe pasture (John 10:3-4).

I am struck with how nurturing and gentle a shepherd must be. He is keenly aware of his sheep's needs. He accepts their capacities. He doesn't push them beyond their limits or neglect their essential necessities. Instead, a shepherd surveys the landscape, looking for the best possible place to lead his sheep in order to provide for them.

A shepherd is also tuned in to the individuality of each sheep. He can look out over a vast flock and identify each one by name. His knowing of them is a familiar, intimate knowing of each marking and blemish, each curve of the ear and contour of the nose, the timbre of each bleating voice.

How contrary that is to the way we envision God. Often we think all God cares about is what he can get from us. Our portrait of God looks more like that of a heavy-handed taskmaster who is never quite satisfied with the service we render, one who is always asking for more, taking more, and rationing what he gives in return.

Yet time and again in the Bible, God is defined as a shepherd who *gives* to *us*. This shepherd-sheep relationship is one of utter dependence, where the shepherd gives and the sheep receives, where God offers us tender care and we take it in.

We are not nameless and faceless to God, but ones he knows thoroughly and personally. How significant that the Bible tells us that God shepherds each of us as an individual—one whose name he knows, one whose soul he is concerned for, one whose capacity he accepts, one whose needs matter to him.

The Second Image: A Shepherd Who Rescues His Lost Sheep

Imagine you hear the weak, pitiful bleating of a small sheep. There, over the ledge and into the thorny brambles she has fallen. The cliff is steep and she is unable to secure her footing. Her shepherd hears the bleating and leans precariously over the ledge, staff in hand. He stretches himself out, craning his body, reaching for her. A vulture flies overhead—an opportunist, waiting. The sheep's eyes meet her shepherd's. He is determined to reach her and save her. Beads of sweat break out on the shepherd's brow; with one final thrust he takes hold of her, not with his crook but with his hand. He pulls her gently but firmly to safety, securely in his embrace. Take a moment and meditate on this image in your mind.

It may not be a stretch to envision a shepherd going out after a lost sheep like this one. But it takes some imagination to envision God being that determined to pursue us when we become lost. Yet that is exactly how God is described. Listen to these words from Ezekiel:

> "I myself will search for my sheep and look after them. As a shepherd looks after his scattered flock when he is with them, so will I look after my sheep. I will rescue them from all the places where they were scattered on a day of clouds and darkness. I will bring

them out from the nations and gather them from the countries, and I will bring them into their own land." (Ezekiel 34:11-13)

Jesus told a parable that reinforces this story. He compared himself to a shepherd who left the ninety-nine sheep in his fold to go after one lost sheep and find her.

What We Discover About Ourselves in This Landscape

Prone to Wander, Lord, I Feel It!

We discover our need for the green pastures when we are lost and have wandered away from home. Have you ever felt lost inside yourself or plagued by an inner restlessness? Sometimes it's intense and unrelenting, as though your soul is chafing like a wild horse in a corral. Other times it is more sub-liminal, an agitation concealed as if behind some hedge in your heart. Either way, the sensation persists, this restless feeling and an urge to wander. We yearn for and enter the green pastures when we have come face-to-face with the prone-to-wander inclinations of our heart.

Most of us are cognizant of an underlying force that keeps drawing us off-kilter and away from God and the moorings of our true heart. When Jesus asked his disciples if they were going to leave him, Peter told Jesus, "Lord, to whom shall we go? You have the words of eternal life" (John 6:68). And yet a short time later Peter denied Jesus three different times, claiming that he never even knew him.

Residing in each of us is a potpourri of conflicting, contradictory, and opposing voices. We desperately need the environment of the green pastures to sort through the tangles of these conflicting conversations. This landscape provides a place where we can listen more deeply to the voice of God our shepherd and to the voice of our true self, the person he created us to be.

This tendency to wander has been around a long time. "Come, Thou Fount of Every Blessing," a hymn written in 1758 by Robert Robinson, describes this inner nagging that is common to all humanity.

> O to grace how great a debtor
>   daily I'm constrained to be!
> Let thy goodness, like a fetter,
>   bind my wandering heart to thee.
> Prone to wander, Lord, I feel it,
>   prone to leave the God I love;
> here's my heart, O take and seal it,
>   seal it for thy courts above.

What We Discover About God in This Landscape

A Shepherd Who Speaks in a Voice We Recognize

When the storms of life come along and frighten us, or we simply wander from God and the bent of our own soul, our shepherd notices and promises to come looking for us. He says, "I myself will search for my sheep and look after them. I will leave the ninety-nine and go out after the one who is lost." In the green pastures, we discover that God is a shepherd who knows when we have lost our North Star and sets out on a mission to help us find our way back home.

But practically speaking, *how* does he rescue us and show us our way back home? Jesus said one of the ways is through speaking to us in a voice we recognize. He said that he will call his own sheep by name and lead them out, and his sheep will follow him because *they know his voice* (John 10:4). This voice, coming through the intercom of our spiritual sensitivities, should register as *his* voice. We should be able to distinguish it from all the other voices vying for our attention.

But that's just the problem. We don't distinguish his voice

because of all the other voices that are clamoring inside our heads. So often it is hard to know which voice belongs to him and which are the voices of our upbringing, insecurities, and fears.

The voices we hear can be the voices of our false selves prodding us to continue obeying their demands. One of my false voices is my people-pleasing voice. Sometimes I will hear things like, "You better call her back or she will be mad at you." "You better win him over or he won't like you." I don't always recognize the origin of these nagging voices that fuel my energies toward trying to keep everybody happy with me.

These clamoring voices draw us away from God and our own true heart. *They incite us to wander.* But it is the voice of God that calls us back home, to a place of rest, where we can experience a peace-filled soul. It is imperative that we settle down into the green pastures in order to filter out those voices and start listening to the voice of our shepherd.

Jesus spoke confidently that his voice was one his sheep would recognize. Taken at face value, that means that when we stop and listen, we will know when he is speaking. He has given us what we need, the spiritual sensitivity, to discern his voice. Paul described our capacity to hear God's voice in this way:

> For who among men knows the thoughts of a man except the man's spirit within him? In the same way no one knows the thoughts of God except the Spirit of God. We have not received the spirit of the world but the Spirit who is from God, that we may understand what God has freely given us. (1 Corinthians 2:11-12)

God has given us his spirit so that we understand his voice, and he knows exactly how to speak in a way that we recognize and with a means we comprehend. He knows exactly how to get through to us: the thoughts that will make sense, the signs that we will notice, the experiences that have meaning to us. That's why we can have confidence in our ability to hear him speak and discern what he is saying to us.

I have found that his voice is often quiet and calm, his words simple but resonating with wisdom and truth. When I am seeking his presence and guidance and become quiet, his still, small voice has a chance to register. Once his thoughts come into my mind and I consider them, I will have a strong confirmation, a resonance inside me, that these words are from him.

The solitude of the green pastures is essential in order to still the noise in our souls and begin to distinguish the voice of God, our shepherd. That is one of its virtues: the ability to reacquaint us with God's voice and help us listen to what he has to say.

Speaking Through the Voice of His Persistent Love

Not long ago, I attended a Christian twelve-step meeting. I went to hear my nephew share his story of how God had persistently pursued him for more than fifteen years while he lost himself in a lifestyle of drug and alcohol abuse. Danny told how his life was spiraling downward, how he was consuming lethal quantities of alcohol, popping pills, smoking pot, snorting cocaine, and gambling. Not only was he a user, he was also a seller. Not only was he a gambler, he was also a bookie.

On top of all that, he began to dabble in the occult. He told how, more than fifteen years ago in the middle of the night, he had called me—his "Christian" aunt—while he was drunk and reading the Bible. I remembered it well. He told me on the phone that he had a friend who was into "some black stuff." Little did I know, so was he.

Afterward, I wrote him a letter and shared my story: how I had felt ashamed of many choices I had made and thought God was ashamed of me as well. But quietly, God kept drawing me to himself. Then one day, I cried out with all of my being and gave my life to Christ.

During the meeting, Danny pulled out the letter and read it to the group. He said that throughout his reckless wandering he kept the letter close to him, reading it whenever his thoughts turned toward God. God's voice, speaking through Danny's growing spiritual sensitivity, began to register, until finally one day he gave in to the persistent love of God.

Who Keeps Whom?

As I reflect on God's love for us, I am struck with the awareness that most of us don't *really* believe that God is keeping us close to himself. Instead, we carry on as if we are the ones who must keep ourselves close to God. Our diligent devotion is all too often fueled by the fear that if we don't keep up our end of the bargain, we will become lost from God, drifting far from his reach.

Though we must respond to his pursuit and not resist his rescue, God makes a promise to stand guard over us, actively wooing us from wandering away from him: "Once you were wandering like lost sheep. But now you have turned to your Shepherd, the Guardian of your souls" (1 Peter 2:25 NLT).

The Third Image: A Shepherdess Who Heals Her Hurting Sheep

Picture a shepherdess, crouched over a small lamb, gently pressing her hand to its heart. She studies his injuries—gouges from the teeth of a predator—and touches the lamb's ears, rubbing them softly. The horn of oil slung over her shoulder is uncapped. She pours a small amount into the wound and then takes a cloth and cleans it. Tearing strips of the cloth, she binds up the deep gashes in the sheep's flesh, careful not to inflict more pain. Cooing softly, she speaks gently to her patient, assuring him that she is there and that everything will be all right. Behind her are the steep hills of the grazing pasture. The sun is setting. A small light shines far away in the distance. Night is falling, so she will wait, lying beside her little one till morning comes. Take a moment to meditate on this image in your mind.

In Ezekiel 34:15-16, God describes himself as a healer of our wounds: "I myself will tend my sheep and have them lie down. . . . I will bind up the injured and strengthen the weak." When the storms of life hit, we can become lost and wounded. We are hurt by people, roughed up by adversity, beaten down by strains and stresses. And when we are, God tells us that he longs to be a shepherd who binds up our injuries and helps us regain our strength.

What We Discover About Ourselves in This Landscape

We All Are Wounded and Need Healing

Some of our hurts can be seen. Many of them cannot. They are covered up by our well-dressed, high-performance, over-achieving personas. Our injuries can be physical, emotional, mental, or spiritual. No matter what type, they can impair us from becoming more whole as individuals and from living in healthy, loving relationship with others. Until we become aware of our wounds and need for healing, we won't permit God to tend our wounds.

Spending time in the green pastures provides the opportunity to become acquainted with some of our hurts and God's desire to heal them. Our time there helps us recognize our wounds and learn how we live out of our wounds and inflict injury to others because of our woundedness. This time of quiet reflection affords us the chance to take an honest look at ourselves and let God into our broken, bleeding hearts.

Letting God into Our Wounded Places

How do we let God into that wounded place to heal it? Today the prevailing teaching on healing suggests that the main way God heals or changes us is through healing the way we think. Though that is part of healing, I don't think it is all *or* enough.

Over the past several years, I have become more aware of my own formative childhood wounds. There is much I am thankful for related to the love and nurture of my parents. At the same time, I am aware of the impact of growing up in a home with a very domineering father. He was a bully who often humiliated and belittled both me and my mother. When he saw weakness or vulnerability, he would expose and ridicule it. Needless to say, in that environment it wasn't very safe to be a child, let alone the only girl and the baby of the family.

I was wounded from that experience. As a result, I internalized my dad's humiliation, felt deep fear and shame and the need to hide my weak, childish, sensitive self. So, I worked hard to be strong and capable in order to avoid humiliation. Becoming an adult, I began to notice that when I saw weakness or felt bullied or intimidated, I would live out of my wound and belittle and intimidate in return.

Through my reaction to some painful experiences over the past several years, I have become more cognizant of this deep wound. Through spiritual direction, counseling, and healing prayer, God, my shepherd, has begun to heal the wounds in my heart.

All three experiences have been integral to God healing my wounds. Spiritual direction has helped me understand the significance of the events in my life that triggered my wounds and how God is involved in my life through them. Counseling has helped expose some warped thinking and identify the false selves I had developed to cover up my wounds and make my life work. And healing prayer has brought those painful childhood memories to the surface and given God the opportunity to touch them with his tender love and healing presence.

What We Discover About God in This Landscape

God's Healing Ways

God desires to bring healing to our broken, wounded lives. He is able to when we let his healing presence into the places where we are in pain and broken. We are all wounded lambs who need our shepherd's healing touch to recover and become more whole and healthy people. In order to heal, we must let him in to access those wounds and do what only he can do.

During our rest in the green pastures of life, we discover God's healing ways. It is important to understand the different ways in which God heals. There are certainly many outlandish and deceptive notions about how God heals. But it is important to know that God still does heal and to understand the ways he does his healing work in our lives. There are at least three types of healing described in Scripture.

Healing in an Instant

The first type of healing that comes to mind is from the stories of Jesus when he healed those who were blind, afflicted with disease, disabled, and enslaved. In a word, with a touch, in a command, Jesus healed them instantly, and he continues to heal instantly today.

I might not be so confident about this if it weren't for my own personal experience. It happened one summer during college when I was studying music near Paris, France. I woke up one morning with a debilitating migraine headache and was in a frustrating quandary. That day I had planned to go with some other students to do some sightseeing. Though I felt awful, I decided to chance it and go.

Our first stop was the Cathedral of Notre Dame. As we walked around the inner perimeter of the cathedral, my head was pounding and I felt nauseated. I could barely shuffle along with the crowd, the pain was so intense. Then, as I flanked the right side of the sanctuary, an old, tattered-looking peasant caught my eye. He was seated in one of the pews, his immense, worn hands folded over his face.

I gazed at him and intuitively felt something of his pain. Honestly, I was more drawn to this man than to the remarkable architecture of that place. For a moment, I totally forgot myself and was filled with a deep love in my heart for him. My mind lingered in prayer.

We exited the cathedral into the beautiful morning sun, got in our car, and headed to our next site. Suddenly, I realized that my headache was completely gone! I had a vague trace of its memory, but the bulk of it had been lifted instantly. The only explanation I have is that God healed me. Whether our wounds be physical, emotional, or spiritual, God is capable of healing them in an instant.

Healing as a Process

God can and does heal instantly. But sometimes he does his healing work through time and process. The Old Testament story of Ruth and Naomi is one of those occasions. Naomi became a bitter, broken woman because of the death of her husband and sons. Being a widow and childless made her the most vulnerable, helpless individual in society. In fact, she changed her name to Mara, which means bitter. But over time, God took care of Naomi through her daughter-in-law, Ruth. This devoted young woman became God's angel of rescue, providing for Naomi's livelihood and continuing her lineage through marrying Naomi's relative. As a result, over a period of time, God healed Naomi of her bitter and blaming heart.

Many of our emotional and spiritual wounds are healed over time, as we experience God's love and grace personally and through others in our community. The alchemy of love plus grace plus time has a powerful healing effect on our hearts.

Healing Through the Gift of Grace

The third type of healing is illustrated in the story of Paul, who asked God to heal him of a physical problem. He more than likely had an eye disease, and Paul asked God three times to heal it. Finally, God responded and said: "My grace is sufficient for you, for my power is made perfect in weakness" (2 Corinthians 12:9). Instead of healing Paul's wound in the traditional sense, God gave him unusual grace to endure the condition.

Have you ever known people like that? They have a condition

that would seem unbearable, and yet they handle it with such grace and dignity. That's how I would describe a woman I know who has battled breast cancer on and off for fifteen years. Four times it has come back. And each time she goes through the full gamut of chemotherapy and radiation. She has her bad days. But overall, this woman keeps her chin up, is truly grateful for her life, and lives with amazing courage and grace.

Through an instant, over time, or by offering unusual grace, God does his healing work in our lives. How it happens can be difficult to explain. There are steps we take and work we do. There are distorted thoughts to uproot and God's truth to implant. But when it's all said and done, we look at what has happened and have to confess that God is a shepherd who heals us, often from the inside out.

Life Skills

One would think that settling down into such a lush landscape would come naturally. But the truth is, we have to learn some important life skills in order to garner all that the green pastures have to offer. The following are some practices that will help you experience the rest and healing you may need for your weary, lost, and wounded soul.

Resting

In this landscape we learn to rest: to cease striving and be still. Because most of us have a resistance to rest, we must learn to press through the anxiety and discomfort that we feel in order to get to a place of rest.

Practically speaking, rest can take on lot of expressions:
- Rest from work
- Rest from TV, radio, computer—any form of technology
- Rest from certain habits, like tennis, golf, or shopping; anything that might be an obsession

- Rest from certain spiritual practices (I have a friend who rested for a time from church, the Bible, and small groups—in order to draw near to God.)

Resting simply means taking a break from what you have been doing. It can last a day or a long afternoon; or it can be for an extended time, involving weeks or months.

Distinguishing God's Voice

When we respond to the invitation to rest in the green pastures, the quiet often gives us space for the other voices in our life to quiet down. Through extended times of being with our shepherd, we begin to distinguish his voice more clearly.

- If you struggle to hear from God and to know your own heart, it may have a lot to do with not taking time in the green pastures to listen.
- Practice sitting in silence, keeping your attention focused on Christ, in an attentive posture of listening.
- Learn to listen from that deeper place in you where God's spirit resides.
- As you sit in silence, write down whatever thoughts, impressions, or pictures come to mind.
- Always compare what you hear with the spirit of God's word: God is love, and if you have heard God's voice, it will be a voice of love.

Being Gentle and Patient with Ourselves

Spending time with God in the green pastures of life helps us remember that we are human, limited, vulnerable people. Remembering that helps us honor our limits, pay attention to the needs of our heart, and take care of ourselves as we let God take care of us.

- One practical way to tend to the needs and hurts in your own heart is through taking time for yourself.
- Take a personal day, blocking out time to be alone without any responsibility or distractions.

- Your heart knows what it needs to be nourished and restored. Listen to what sounds good or refreshing to you.
- Respond and act on what comes to mind. Eat when you feel like eating; nap when you feel like napping. Take a walk, visit an art museum, listen to music, sketch, sit and do nothing, sip tea, eat chocolate.
- Respond to anything that sounds like a gift. It is one of the ways you will become reacquainted with your own heart's desires.

There Are Mountains to Climb

A few years ago, I met a remarkable woman. Her name is Jean Deeds. One Sunday morning while reading the paper, Jean read an article about a person who had hiked the entire Appalachian Trail—all 2,155 miles of it. Something about that idea awakened a longing in Jean, a longing that she acted upon.

Within a few months, Jean quit a great job and began making plans and training to hike the trail herself. She started out in March of 1994, at the age of fifty-one, to hike the entire length of the trail alone! Her book, *There Are Mountains to Climb*, is a wonderful memoir of her experiences on the trail.

Jean told me something that I will never forget. She said that for years she drew from the solace her journey had forged in her. Jean said that for a very long time she experienced a palpable and abiding sense of peace and tranquility that all those months alone on the trail had created.

Jean is one of my heroes. I admire her because she heeded the call inside herself: the call to come away to the green pastures (or the Appalachian Trail) and find rest for her weary soul.

Many of us today are living with such small, shriveled-up souls because we have been unwilling to heed the call. The green pastures are a replenishing landscape from which to awaken our souls and be restored. Our shepherd has sent the invitation. He is simply waiting for us to accept.

For Reflection and Conversation

• When have you spent time in the green pastures during your past journey with God? Describe that time.

• Why do you find it difficult to rest?

• Think of a time when you were lost or wandering from yourself or from God. How did God pursue you as your shepherd? Describe that experience.

• For what reasons do you need to turn toward the green pastures right now? What will it take for you to make that choice?

• Describe what it is like for you to listen to God's voice. What is getting in the way of your hearing him? Are you aware of anything he might be saying to you right now?

Chapter Six

THE LAND OF EXILE

Genesis 37–50

IN THE FIRST SCENE OF THE MOVIE *THE UPSIDE OF ANGER* *(2005)*, a woman named Terry, played by Joan Allen, is present at the graveside burial of her husband. A sea of black umbrellas forms a canopy over the assembly of mourners. There is a somber flatness to the mood. Flanked on either side of Terry are her four daughters, and you hear the narrator, her youngest daughter, tell the story of her mother's exiled life. Here is her description.

> A case in point in anger's ability to change us is my mother.
>
> My mother was always the nicest person I ever knew. She was the nicest, sweetest woman anybody who ever knew her ever knew.
>
> Then things changed ... and she changed. She got angry. Good and angry.
>
> Anger has turned my mother into a very sad and bitter woman. If she wasn't my mother, I'd slap her. I would. I'd look her straight in the face and tell her what I really think of her. And then I'd run really fast in the opposite direction.

Terry was exiled from the life that had been hers. The loss of her husband transported her to some foreign reality in a faraway land. It was as though she woke up to someone else's existence and had to don another's life, a life she never wanted to wear. Now life dripped with rainy days as a black cloud of anger and bitterness settled over her being, apparently for good.

The land of exile is a time, like Terry's, when we feel cut off, displaced, out of sync with the life we thought was ours. We become separated, either from the life that *was* ours or from the life we *thought* would be ours. And the life we have inherited feels like a poor fit.

Our heart yearns for a time when we felt at home with our surroundings and ourselves. Exiled from our dreams, we are left with a truth we find so disappointing or unbelievable that we can't imagine ever reconciling ourselves to it. The land of exile is the opposite of the promised land, and similar but distinct from the desert landscape. In the desert, we are most conscious of the hole that has been left from loss. In the land of exile, we are most conscious of what has replaced the hole— an ill-fitting, irreconcilable life.

The Very First Exile

The story of Adam and Eve is the first incident of exile in our human history. Their idyllic life in a garden home was short-lived. Banished from paradise by not following the house rules, they were turned out into a land made of stubborn soil that would require toil in order to glean its bounty.

How bewildered they must have felt when they encountered difficulties in the soil of their new destiny: land that would not till, thorns and thistles that punctured their thumbs, weather that worked against them. Even relationally, there was a new, disturbing dynamic. Tension rubbed them raw as they set to work, sweat on their brows, cultivating their newly acquired life in a land of exile.

The Death of Dreams, the Path of Exile

We find ourselves in the land of exile when our dreams are smothered or dashed; when our longings are withheld from us; *when the life we thought was ours is exchanged for a foreign life in a foreign land.*

Here are some common paths that lead toward exile:

- People who dreamed that they would be married for life and end up widowed or divorced
- Couples who dreamed of becoming parents and live with the ache of empty arms
- Individuals who dreamed of being married and, year after year, yearn for a companion, but remain single
- Those who have lost jobs and languish in want of a new one
- Christ-followers who dreamed of being a strong Christian family and are heartbroken as their spouse or children reject Christ
- Parents who dreamed of raising healthy, happy kids and now live with the trauma of the death, estrangement, or injury of a child
- Those who dreamed that life would be one way and are now living with the realization that it will never be that way

I think of some friends of mine who adopted a beautiful little girl. She was born with several heart problems and as a result went through numerous heart surgeries and hospitalizations. The first few years of life were a very rocky road. As she grew, it was obvious that she had some developmental delay. Thinking it was due to her rough start, they tried to be patient. But over time, they began to wonder if there was something more.

After many doctor's visits and tests, their daughter was diagnosed with a rare chromosomal abnormality. As a result, she will never function as an independent adult, live on her own, hold a job, or marry. Though her parents have responded with tremendous grace and courage, they are living a life they never expected they would live. They are in the land of exile.

A Young Man with Big Dreams

I also think of Joseph in the Old Testament, a young man who had big dreams, dreams so big that they got him in trouble. And he spent thirteen years in exile before he saw any sign of redemption on the skyline of his life.

One day young Joseph shared his big dreams with his brothers and father. And that's when all his troubles began. First, he told his brothers of the dream where all their sheaves of grain bowed down to his sheaf. (That went over well!) Then he told his brothers and father his second dream: that the sun and moon and eleven stars were bowing down to him.

His father rebuked him, saying, "Will your mother and I and your brothers actually come and bow down to the ground before you?" (Genesis 37:10). His brothers seethed with anger and jealousy. But his father, we are told, kept the matter in his mind.

Perhaps Joseph grew up believing he was special; maybe he had some sense of his destiny. After all, he was the favored son of Jacob. That was evident to all his brothers by the finely decorated robe that his father had made just for him. As a result, Joseph's dreams provoked them, and they began planning to deport the young stargazer.

Hatred brewing in their hearts, his brothers boiled with bitter resentment toward Joseph. Soon after, during a visit from Joseph while they were tending their father's flocks, they ganged up on him, stripped him of his colorful robe, sold him to a traveling caravan as a slave, and told their father that a wild animal had eaten him. The caravan ended up in Egypt, where Joseph spent thirteen years in exile before he ever saw any substantial hope in his life.

When we, like Joseph, dwell in the land of exile, we know that we are far away from home. Our heart tells us of its homesickness as we dream of the life we had thought would be ours.

What We Discover About Ourselves in This Landscape

For thirteen years, Joseph lived in Egypt. His brothers' betrayal and his subsequent exile were only the first of many difficult battles that Joseph would face. In fact, we know very little of how he processed his exile. But an event in Genesis 41 provides a shaft of light into Joseph's inner world.

After several years and several setbacks, Joseph had the opportunity to meet with Pharaoh, the king of Egypt, to interpret a troubling dream of Pharaoh's. Joseph did so, predicting seven years of abundance and then seven years of famine. Pharaoh was deeply impressed and placed Joseph in charge of the entire country to prepare for the times to come.

Soon after, at the age of thirty, Joseph became a father. He had two sons whom he named Manasseh and Ephraim. Manasseh means "God has made me forget all my trouble and all my father's household." And Ephraim means "God has made me fruitful in the land of my suffering" (Genesis 41:51-52).

Isn't it interesting that after thirteen years, Joseph still framed his life in relation to his brothers' betrayal and the suffering that had come as a result?

A Brawl with Bitterness

Joseph's story suggests to me that one of the responses he had, and we may have, to the land of exile was to brawl with bitterness. Bitterness is a response we have to someone who has harmed us or to something that has happened to us that is difficult to accept.

By definition, *bitterness* means holding onto or showing feelings of intense animosity, resentment, or vindictiveness. For thirteen years, Joseph held onto and nursed the wounds of his brothers' betrayal. Bitterness isn't an isolated feeling but a *condition, a state of being.* And when we are bitter, we often blame the event or person who is most responsible for our exile. Think back to Terry in the movie *The Upside of Anger.* She was bitter and consequently blamed her dead husband for leaving her and making life miserable.

A Root of Bitterness

How do you know the difference between an *isolated* angry, bitter feeling and the *condition* of bitterness? The Bible uses the image of a root to describe the way this attitude gets lodged inside us. It says, "See to it that no one misses the grace of God and that no bitter root grows up to cause trouble and defile many" (Hebrews 12:15).

When bitterness is ingested, it takes root and grows down deep into the bedrock of our souls. As a result, a poisonous vine propagates, infiltrating our lives, contaminating the way we view all of life, and sullying almost everyone we meet.

I think of an invasive groundcover we planted in our garden. We didn't realize what we were planting, and consequently it began aggressively to infiltrate. No matter how well I weeded, it kept cropping up everywhere. Now, the third summer after its removal, it's still showing up in several nooks and crannies of my flower bed.

That's how it is with bitterness. Anger and resentment become rooted in our hearts and begin to turn up everywhere in our lives and relationships.

Bitterness is the consequence we experience when we don't properly grieve our disappointments and losses. Whenever we experience loss and are exiled from the life we hoped would be ours, we go through stages of grief. One of the early stages is anger. Anger is a natural, human response to loss. But sometimes we get stuck in anger, and the result is bitterness.

Why do you suppose we get stuck in anger? For many, we often prefer anger to sadness, hurt, and disappointment because it makes us feel more powerful and in control. But we don't always notice that as we nurture our anger, over time we become bitter, unwilling to accept what has happened.

I once read that you can tell you are bitter if you hang on to a negative memory with precise, distinct detail. Bitter people are ones who can recall a negative conversation they had with someone five years ago with exact wording and inflections. Why? Because they have rehashed the conversation over and over and over again.

Why, after thirteen years, was Joseph still so mindful of the pain of his exile? I suspect that it was because he had rehashed what had happened to him repeatedly and wrestled with a bitter spirit.

The Time It Takes to Heal

The single most painful event of my life up until now has been an experience of exile. My husband and I had been in ministry for a number of years at a megachurch, a place where we had given our hearts fully, were deeply connected in community, and were living fruitful lives. After major restructuring and staff layoffs, some personal conflict with individuals, and a disappointing conclusion to a yearlong dialogue on women in ministry, my husband and I resigned.

We had envisioned serving in this church for the rest of our professional lives. We didn't see the end coming. Suddenly, at the age of almost fifty, we found ourselves living as refugees from the life that had been ours.

One of my greatest concerns and most difficult battles has been the bitterness in my own heart toward individuals who were hurtful to us. I admit that the battle is not over. I struggle with reliving, rehashing, and sustaining bitterness toward people who were wounding. As with the battle in my garden, I have needed to uproot the cynical, vindictive attitudes I have had toward them and weed those feelings out of my heart. Some days I do better than others.

One thing that Joseph's story and mine have taught me is the fact that it takes time to heal from the wounds that provoke bitterness. If we long for deep transformation and deep healing, it will take time and God's tender care to work through all the issues of disappointment and disillusionment that have led to our exile. Weeding is hard work. But if left undone, bitterness is a toxic sin that will choke the life from our souls.

What We Discover About God in This Landscape

I know what it is like to have to contend with an insidious weed that has deep and invasive roots. The land of exile is a dangerous place because we wrestle with the invasive root of bitterness. But we are not left alone in our struggle, because we have the opportunity to discover some vital insights about God.

God's Willingness to Let the Pain of Life Hurt Us

As we consider our exile and Joseph's, the place we have to begin is the acknowledgment that this landscape reveals God's willingness to allow pain, injustice, unfairness, and cruelty to disrupt our lives. When I read about Joseph, that is what is so apparent in his story.

Joseph is not only sold as a slave by his brothers and exiled to Egypt but also, some time later, thrown into jail on false charges that he molested his boss's wife. Consequently, Joseph, an innocent man, remains in jail for several years. Then, after helping two other prisoners who were released from jail, Joseph is forgotten by them when they could have helped secure his release.

Time after time, we see Joseph experience setbacks in his life. Each one registers as further exile from the life that should have been his. Yet, lying right beside the unfairness, injustice, unkindness, and cruelty was God!

God's Ability to Work in the Midst of Our Exile

Each time Joseph encountered a painful situation or discouraging blow, he was met with not only the impact of that event but also the generous and gracious presence of God embedded in the event! Here are some examples:

The providence of God would have Joseph sold to a man

named Potiphar, who was a generous man and was responsive to God's spirit. While in Potiphar's house,

> The LORD was with Joseph and he prospered, and he lived in the house of his Egyptian master. When his master saw that the LORD was with him and that the LORD gave him success in everything he did, Joseph found favor in his eyes and became his attendant. Potiphar put him in charge of his household, and he entrusted to his care everything he owned. (Genesis 39:2-4)

Then Potiphar's wife tried to seduce Joseph. When he shunned her advances, she accused him of trying to rape her, so Potiphar had Joseph thrown into jail. But once again he encountered a generous benefactor. "But while Joseph was there in the prison, the LORD was with him; he showed him kindness and granted him favor in the eyes of the prison warden. So the warden put Joseph in charge of all those held in the prison, and he was made responsible for all that was done there" (Genesis 39:20-22).

Finally, when Joseph interpreted Pharaoh's puzzling dream, he was made overseer of Egypt and saved the Egyptians and his own family from starvation. This time Joseph recognized what was happening. He told his brothers, "You intended to harm me, but God intended it for good to accomplish what is now being done, the saving of many lives" (Genesis 50:20).

Joseph's story illustrates the troubling reality that a lot of the things that happen to us are neither of God nor of his desire. Even more perplexing, God doesn't step in and stop them from happening. He doesn't protect us from exile.

Nothing about Joseph's betrayal, his imprisonment, or his exile was instigated by God. God didn't sanction any of the wrong; but he did show up in the midst of it! He worked alongside it!

A Theology of God and Evil

The story of Joseph has provided for me a window of insight into some disturbing questions of life, such as *What does it mean that God is sovereign, when there is so much pain, evil, wrong, and cruelty in the world? How do the two—God and evil—coexist?*

I don't know how you have resolved such questions for yourself. And I am in no position to offer a thorough discussion on the topic or present a clear case one way or the other. But Joseph's story has helped me see that, in spite of the troubling, devastating, and awful things that happen, God is not limited, hindered, or confined by them. He doesn't participate in the evil. He doesn't cause the wrong. He doesn't sanction the cruelty. *But he does show up in the midst, right beside it all.*

That realization seems so much more honest and generous to me than trying to "fit" evil into some category *under* the sovereignty of God. Evil is evil. And God is blameless. But the good news is that whatever evil is done in the world, God's ability to work in our lives is not thwarted by it. He works in, among, through, and in spite of all that is flawed in this world.

God's Redemption in Spite of All That Goes Wrong

It took time for Joseph to sort through the rubble of his exiled life. But as he did, he began to get a perspective about God that was both accurate and truthful, one that offered him hope.

Because of severe famine in the region, twice Joseph's brothers had to come to Egypt from Israel to get grain. After his brothers' second trip to Egypt, Joseph revealed his identity to them. Of course, they were terrified and assumed that he would use his authority to punish them and exile them as they did him. But his response was really remarkable. He told them,

"Come close to me." When they had done so, he said, "I am your brother Joseph, the one you sold into Egypt! And now, do not be distressed and do not be angry with yourselves for selling me here, because it was to save lives that God sent me ahead of you.... God sent me ahead of you to preserve for you a remnant on earth and to save your lives by a great deliverance.

"So then, it was not you who sent me here, but God." (Genesis 45:4-5, 7-8)

Wow! For thirteen years, Joseph battled bitterness toward his brothers and his exiled life. But at some point God freed his heart to forgive them and to recognize God's redemptive involvement over the affairs of his life. Joseph didn't excuse his mistreatment or deny his brothers' wrongdoing. But Joseph recognized God's overriding presence and purposes.

Joseph told them, "It was not you who sent me here, but God." Can you imagine being able to say that to the perpetrator of your exile? Probably not, at least not until you are able to see God work resourcefully and redemptively in your exile. God has an incredible talent for turning bad things around for good. In our exiled lives, we are invited to look earnestly for redemption through God.

For No Good Reason

But what if you don't ever see God's purposes, God's redemptive powers, or God's reasons for why your life didn't turn out as you had hoped?

What if you never understand why you didn't marry, didn't have babies, or had to resign, or why your life turned out as it did? Honestly, I don't think we always know. And that is very, very hard.

The best solace I have found are the words of Romans 8:18: "I consider that our present sufferings are not worth comparing with the glory that will be revealed in us." Someday our present sufferings will seem insignificant when we see what God has done in our lives through them. There are some things in our lives that will never make sense on this side of heaven.

Life Skills

When our dreams have been crushed and we wake up to a reality that is hard to swallow, we learn to take a day at a time and to develop some agility in navigating life. In the land of exile we are far from home. But like visitors to a different culture, we can learn a new language and invaluable new skills that will help us navigate this landscape.

Offering Our True Selves

As we peruse the life of Joseph, we see that he certainly experienced his share of upsets. But one thing that stands out in each frame of his story is how he lived out of the gifts God had placed in him and offered his true self in each and every situation. When we experience a time of exile, we will feel out of place, not at home in ourself or our surroundings.

- In this foreign place, learn to offer your true self.
- Remember who you are, what you are good at, and what you love to do; pursue opportunities to offer those things.
- Dig down deep into your true self and live out of the resources and passions that flow from the person God created you to be.

Learning to Forgive

The second life skill we learn in this landscape is to forgive those who have contributed to our exile. That is more easily said than done. I suspect that Joseph battled the desire for revenge almost every day of his life while in exile, until he began to see redemption taking shape.

- Pay attention to any shred of goodness that you see coming to you or others as a result of your exile.
- Let go of the small vocation of harboring bitterness, in exchange for the generous opportunity to be used by God to bless others' lives.
- Do not exact retribution; seek instead, by the grace of

God, to forgive those who have contributed to your exile.

Letting Go of Bitterness Toward God

The truth is, sometimes the one we are most bitter toward is God. When we find ourselves disappointed and dismayed with life, we often direct our anger and resentment toward God. We don't always realize or give ourselves the freedom to admit that we are really miffed at God.

- If you are angry with God, you need—as strange as it may sound—to work through your "forgiveness" of God, admitting that you feel he has let you down and let you be hurt.
- Seek the help of a friend, pastor, counselor, or spiritual director to pray with you and for you as you release any anger or bitterness in your heart toward God or others.

The Glimpse of a New Vista

As my husband and I embarked on our journey through the land of exile, we began to glimpse a new vista. Though our hearts were broken and we had grieved the life that was ours, we began to see a new life taking shape.

For us, we found the resulting wide open spaces of our life to be a true blessing and delight. Our daily rhythms became sweet: morning coffee, walks with our dog, long conversations, and a simpler life. The new landscape gave us time to adjust and listen more closely to those things that stirred our souls. Our marriage deepened, and our companionship became a greater treasure. We began to uncover redemption in the land of our exile.

Sometimes redemption doesn't look like what we'd like it to. It doesn't always mean that what we lost will be restored. We may never return to what had been "home." Sometimes the only redemption we see is the fact that, if we consent to be shaped by this landscape, it will enlarge our heart for God, deepen our connection with our true self, and forge more Christlike character in us.

Expending Misdirected Anger

Let's go back to the movie *The Upside of Anger*. What you may not know unless you have seen the movie is that Terry's husband had disappeared three years prior to his funeral! Terry pulled together the small scraps of information he had left and concluded that her husband had run off with his secretary, who simultaneously had moved back to Sweden.

For three years, Terry lived with a broken heart and was bitter toward her husband. Then one day, as her neighbor was walking in the acreage behind Terry's home, he discovered an old, dangerous, open well. He peered into the well and discovered the body of Terry's husband, who apparently had fallen into the well three years before and died.

For three years, Terry wandered in the land of exile. Life as she had known it had suddenly been snatched away and replaced with a grim and unwelcome reality. And for three years, she spent her misdirected anger and bitterness at the man she *thought* had caused it.

That's often how it is for us when we awaken to life in exile. We expend a lot of energy looking for someone or something to blame for our misery. Years pass before we may know the truth. But there, among the debris, if we will search for it, are some glimmering shards of redemption.

For Reflection and Conversation

- When in your life have you felt that you were living a life you never thought would be yours? Describe that time.

- In what way do you feel that you are living in exile right now?

• Have you ever seen an "upside to anger"? Explain.

• As you inventory your life, for what reasons have you struggled with bitterness? What have you done with the bitterness?

• Is there anyone in your life whom you need to forgive? What would help you forgive that person? What steps can you take to move toward forgiveness?

• In what ways are you seeing God bring blessings from your exiled life?

• What are you learning to offer of yourself in the midst of your exile?

Chapter Seven

THE DEEP WATERS

2 Samuel 11:1–12:25; Psalms 18 and 69

Offering Substitutes

SARAH WAS A REALLY GOOD MOM. SHE WAS VERY CARE-ful, thorough, and diligent in everything she did, especially in her mothering. One day, I sat at her kitchen table as she prepared lunch, meticulously washing, cutting, and arranging fruit and vegetables and cleaning up as she went.

At her feet was Sam, her eighteen-month-old. He was a bit fussy and kept clinging to her legs, whimpering as she continued her preparations. In my mind, I kept waiting for her to pick him up. But instead, she kept working and he kept whining, only now it was beginning to escalate.

At this point I became distracted, wishing that she would scoop up this little bundle and offer him some comfort. Suddenly, she stopped what she was doing, crossed the room, grabbed a blanket, and handed it to him, saying, "Here, Sam, here's your special blanket."

I was surprised and speechless. She had not done anything horrible. But all of a sudden, I saw her action for what it was: she was offering her son a replacement for herself. What he needed was her; what she offered him was a substitute. Unintentionally, she was training her son to bond with an object instead of with her.

Don't get me wrong; I'm not down on special blankets or stuffed animals to provide comfort to children. This was just one of those moments when I saw the tendency to offer substitutes in place of human connection. It awakened me to the times I have done the same thing to my kids and my husband. I offer them a substitute when what they really need is me.

From a young age, all of us learn to find comfort in substitutes. What we really need and yearn for is love, love that can be transmitted only through the kindness and affection of a person, that is, through relationship. But instead, we are given any number of substitutes to pacify us. So, before long we learn to look for, choose, and become dependent on substitutes for love, instead of waiting for the real thing.

When the Water Is Rising over Our Heads

The landscape of deep waters is a time in our lives when we begin to realize that we have become excessively dependent on something: a substitute that we have looked to for comfort to help us feel alive, to feel better about ourselves, to gain control, or to feel more significant. What we are depending on doesn't really give us what we want or need. It only offers us a facsimile, a substitute for the love our hearts ache to know.

We typically don't realize that we are using this substitute to mask our need for love. However, what we do realize is that we are increasingly controlled by our reliance on it. It feels as if we are being pulled down, starting to drown in the rising waters of our compulsiveness. We can't seem to stop the destructive thought pattern, bad habit, or unhealthy dependency.

We enter the landscape of deep waters when we begin to struggle with our unhealthy attachment to substitutes. Powerless, struggling to stay afloat, we try to overcome the force that has us in its grip.

David described the sensation of struggling through the deep waters in this way:

Save me, O God,
  for the waters have come up to my neck.
I sink in the miry depths,
  where there is no foothold.
I have come into the deep waters;
  the floods engulf me.
I am worn out calling for help;
  my throat is parched.
My eyes fail,
  looking for my God. (Psalm 69:1-3)

Compulsions: The Life Preserver of Our False Self

If you've ever spent time in these rumbling waters, you know the sensation of feeling trapped by your obsessions and powerless to escape. Food, control, busyness, vanity, golf, shopping, working, anger, gossiping, approval, performance, achievement, pornography, housekeeping, exercising, relationships, fantasizing—all of these and a host of others can, over time, become compulsive, destructive behaviors that influence our lives, our relationships, and our intimacy with God.

Each object of attachment offers some promise of fulfilling a desire. It offers to reward us in some way, to give us some emotional lift. As David Benner writes, "The most basic function of our compulsions is to help us preserve our false self" (*The Gift of Being Yourself,* p. 85).

Our false self is the person we want others to believe us to be. It is the image we extend to others—what Benner calls our "idealized, public self." We work too much because we want to be seen as competent and successful. We love too much because we want other people to like us and make us feel important. We drink too much because we want to appear more secure and adequate than we feel.

An obsession with sports can make some feel virile. Busyness can offer the illusion of being productive. Shopping, eating, and drinking can give us the sensation of being a happy person. But over time these attachments can begin to yield less and demand more and can become a compulsion that begins to affect and impair our relationships.

Religion Can Be a Compulsion

Even religious activity can become an unhealthy, compulsive attachment. I have seen in myself a tendency to practice certain spiritual disciplines in order to feel all right with myself and God. I have known people who had to participate in certain types of Bible study in order to feel that they were pleasing God and progressing spiritually. I have often wondered if many of us don't form an attachment to the *feeling* we get when we worship, more than to the God we worship.

The fact is that all of us have a tendency to form attachments to things in order to get our needs met by them. It is a universal human phenomenon.

Respected psychiatrist and author Gerald May says, "I am not being flippant when I say that all of us suffer from addiction. Nor am I reducing the meaning of addiction. I mean in all truth that the psychological, neurological, and spiritual dynamics of full-fledged addiction are actively at work within every human being" (*Addiction and Grace*, p. 3).

A Caveat: What Unhealthy Attachments Aren't

Unhealthy attachments and compulsions are not the same as enjoying the simple pleasures of life, things such as a good meal or a new pair of shoes or time with a close friend. Compulsions are those habits, thought patterns, objects, or values that we are so attached to, so dependent on, so controlled by that we are not free to *not* choose them.

When I wake up in the morning and have a cup of coffee, I do not choose it because I am free to choose it; I choose it because if I don't, I will slip into a lethargic stupor, get very grouchy, and have a raging headache.

Honestly, many of our compulsive attachments, such as my attachment to coffee, will not devastate our lives. But some attachments we form will lessen our ability to bond in healthy relationship with God and with others. Each unhealthy habit we have will make it more difficult to know and live out of our true self.

We begin our descent into the landscape of deep waters when we start to struggle with the things to which we have formed unhealthy attachments—when we notice the hurt or pain they cause others, when the thought of losing them becomes terrifying, when we wrestle with living freely out of our true selves but feel bound and controlled by compulsive habits, unable to stop them.

The Story of a Human King

David is described in the Bible as a "man after God's own heart." His passionate love affair with God is recorded in colorful language through many of his psalms. But even King David was very human: he had some unhealthy attachments that became more evident toward the end of his life. One particular episode in his life helps us see this human side of him. And his psalms provide a window into his internal battle with enemies in the deep waters of his soul.

David was a gifted musician and poet who spent most of his adult life as a warrior. If you read his story from beginning to end, it consists of virtually one battle after another, as he fought his own enemies and the enemies of Israel. He was a very passionate, impetuous, emotional man with a tender conscience and a zeal for justice. As the king of Israel, he led with integrity and a genuine fear of God. But then his life story began to snag.

One spring, David decided to stay home from battle: "In the spring, at the time when kings go off to war, David sent Joab out with the king's men and the whole Israelite army" (2 Samuel 11:1). And one evening that spring, when he was restless and couldn't sleep, he took a walk around the roof of his palace and spotted a beautiful, naked woman bathing. And you probably know the rest of the story: "The woman was very beautiful, and David sent someone to find out about her. The man said, 'Isn't this Bathsheba, the daughter of Eliam and the wife of Uriah the Hittite?' Then David sent messengers to get her. She came to him, and he slept with her" (2 Samuel 11:2-4).

What We Discover About Ourselves in This Landscape

We Are Committed to Meeting Our Own Needs

The story reads so seamlessly, doesn't it? It happened just like that: He saw her and he had to have her. There was no pause to reflect or catch himself. He just acted out of some strong inner impulse. Maybe he was restless, bored, or lonely. For some reason he hadn't gone to battle that spring. Whatever he felt, there was a need in his heart that ached. And so David, probably not conscious of this ache, surveyed his life and saw a way to meet his need.

In the landscape of deep waters, we come to understand how profoundly committed we are to meeting our own needs. David acted out of a longing he had for something—maybe intimacy, sexual passion, or beauty. It was almost as though his action was involuntary, as if he hardly noticed what he was doing.

Each of us has that same inclination, that same involuntary reaction when we feel the ache of an unmet longing in our lives. When we need comfort, when we need to feel safe, when we need to feel successful or beautiful, we reach for whatever we can find to fill the need that we have.

The problem isn't that we need these things. The problem is with our commitment to meeting the need *ourselves*, often through the quickest and easiest way we can find.

First Spiritual Flutters

My first memories of recognizing my spiritual need for God took place around the age of fourteen. I lived in the attic of our home;

both my brothers were away at college, and I had the whole place to myself. The attic consisted of a large bedroom, a sitting area with sofa and chairs, a bathroom, and a walk-in closet. I had everything a teenage girl needed to exist in happy oblivion.

And it was in this room that I remember beginning to form some of my first conscious thoughts about God. I began to ask some questions such as *Does God exist?* and *I wonder what he thinks of me?* In my own private utopia I began to acknowledge my interest, curiosity, and desire to know God.

Simultaneously, I also began to notice boys.

For the first time I had a real boyfriend, someone who offered me attention and affection and made me feel something that I longed for: a taste of being known and loved for who I was. Though my spiritual interest was piqued, this easy acquisition of a boy's *facsimile* of love was far too tempting. Over the next several years, and boyfriend after boyfriend, I found myself sliding into a pit of increased emotional dependence and physical involvement that offered a false sense of intimacy.

By the time I reached college, I felt that I had stained my life. I had compromised every vow I had made. I had become a slave to filling this gaping hole in my heart to be loved. I felt powerless to say no to this enemy that now controlled me—an insatiable need for the attention and affection of any young man who would offer it.

Shame from Meeting Our Own Needs

We learn in the landscape of deep waters just how committed we are to meeting our own needs. And then once we begin to meet our needs through compulsive, illegitimate, and harmful ways, we often experience the second characteristic this landscape brings out in us: we feel shame.

Harmful, compulsive substitutes always attack our sense of self-worth. Shame is the ultimate assault. Do you know the sensation of shame? Shame is the internalized belief that there is something wrong with you; that you are worthless, less-than, a defective human being.

Shame might be described as a disgust or loathing of yourself. A person who is bound by shame looks at others and concludes that there is something terribly warped and wrong with themselves, more warped and wrong than with anyone else.

There is something shameful about being controlled by things that are harming us or those we love. We feel shame when we eat a whole bag of potato chips because we are lonely. We feel shame when we have illicit sexual fantasies because our marriage is disappointing. We feel shame when we drink too much at a party because we don't like ourselves and feel ill at ease.

I feel shame when my inner drive to work sways me to neglect my kids or react with irritation at their interruptions. I see the harm I have done to them because I can't control my impulse to stop working when I should and choose to be present with them.

Guilt Mingled with Shame

David experienced genuine guilt over his actions. Not only did he commit adultery with Bathsheba, but as a result she became pregnant with David's baby. In order to cover up his sin and save face, David called Uriah, her husband, home from battle and tried to get him to sleep with Bathsheba. When that plan failed, David had Uriah killed by having him placed on the front lines of the battle.

Psalm 51 is a moving confession of David's guilt over his sin. In it are possible traces of shame. He writes,

> My sin is always before me.
> . . . .
> Surely I was sinful at birth,
>   sinful from the time my mother conceived
>   me.

He begs God, "Do not cast me from your presence / or take your Holy Spirit from me" (vv. 3, 5, 11).

David was obsessed with his own sinfulness; he felt sinful to the core of his being and concluded that he had been so from conception. David worried that God would abandon him because he was so sinful. These statements, though perhaps contrite confessions of guilt, sound an awful lot like shame. And it certainly is reasonable to think that he might have struggled with shame.

In the landscape of deep waters, as we wrestle with the enemies of our soul and see the power we have auctioned to them, shame often begins to soak into our hearts like a stubborn stain. In more than twenty-five years of ministry, I have rarely met anyone who doesn't have issues with shame. Most of the time people don't know that it is shame they are feeling. They just know it is hard to believe that anyone, including God, could love them if they really knew them.

What We Discover About God in This Landscape

God Isn't Put Off Because of Our Sin

It is miserable to be mastered by a compulsive habit and doused with shame. In this landscape of vulnerability and brokenness, we are in a perfect position to experience what God alone can do for us—reach down and rescue us from the troubling waters.

David knew what it was like to feel stuck in a pit, as if he was being swallowed up in quicksand. In Psalm 40, he describes the sensation:

> I waited patiently for the LORD;
>   he turned to me and heard my cry.
> He lifted me out of the slimy pit,
>   out of the mud and mire;
> he set my feet on a rock
>   and gave me a firm place to stand.
> He put a new song in my mouth,
>   a hymn of praise to our God.

Many will see and fear
and put their trust in the LORD. (vv. 1-3)

I love the picture that comes to my mind when I read David's words in Psalm 40. It is a picture of God's strong arms reaching down into a slimy, stinky, filthy pit and pulling David out. In order to do that, God had to get his hands dirty. That's the first thing we discover about God in this landscape: his willingness to *come to us* in our mess and get his hands dirty to save us.

When we are entangled by our compulsive attachments, we often feel stuck, ashamed, and filthy. Familiar voices tell us, "You got yourself into this mess. It's up to you to get yourself out." Because of our dilemma we believe the lie that God wants nothing to do with us, that we have to clean ourselves up before he is willing to respond to our cry. Where does this idea come from?

Have you ever heard someone say, "Because God is holy, he can't have anything to do with sin"? Here's the truth: those most drawn to Jesus, most comfortable in his presence, were the ragged, crusty, hardcore sinners of his day. The religious right were put off by Jesus, ill at ease with his unconventional spirituality. The Pharisees were thrown off-balance by Jesus. But the sinners were right at home.

If God is so put off by sin, then why would blatant sinners find Jesus so compelling? I think we've got it wrong. Jesus was more put off by pretense then he was by an honest sinner. And when we are trapped by the stresses and strongholds of our compulsive personalities, Jesus welcomes us to come to him. He says, "Come to me, all you who are weary and burdened, and I will give you rest" (Matthew 11:28).

If we come to him, we will discover a different reality. Jesus is willing to meet us where we are in order to rescue us. His heart is so responsive—it seems to melt—when we finally hit bottom and the jolt brings us into the full gaze of his eyes. God is near to the brokenhearted and crushed in spirit. He responds with valor and compassion to our emergency calls. He doesn't require us to pull ourselves up by our bootstraps but offers us his hand, to draw us up out of the deep pit and churning waters of our own addictions.

Willpower Is Worthless, but God's Power Can Deliver Us

One of the most counterproductive things we can do when we are in the landscape of deep waters is try to use our own willpower to fight the enemies that are working us over. The premise of the twelve-step program, begun by Alcoholics Anonymous, suggests the same idea. Step one acknowledges a person's powerlessness to help themselves. Step two acknowledges the reality of God (a higher power) and the need to depend on his strength. Sheer willpower won't work in fighting these nagging enemies of the deep.

In the landscape of deep waters we learn that willpower is worthless, but God's power can deliver us from our bondage. When we cry out to God from that deep place of longing, acknowledging our own powerlessness, God is positioned to leverage his power and break the bonds that enslave us.

Most of us know very little of the power of God. We are so busy trying to reform ourselves that we have rarely experienced the delivering power of God to confront the enemies of our soul. David described his own experience of God's power to deliver. In Psalm 18, his song describes the deep waters crashing in around him and the strong, powerful arms of God coming to his aid.

> He reached down from on high and took hold of
> me;
> he drew me out of deep waters.
> He rescued me from my powerful enemy,
> from my foes, who were too strong for
> me.
> They confronted me in the day of my disaster,
> but the LORD was my support.

He brought me out into a spacious place;
he rescued me because he delighted in
me. (vv. 16-19)

The preface to this psalm says that David wrote these words "when the LORD delivered him from the hand of all his enemies and from the hand of Saul." David knew his enemies well. He knew they were too strong for him, and so he confessed that he was powerless. Then he turned to a higher power—to God—for help. God drew him out of the deep waters, overriding David's foes and offering David his full support.

Our trouble is that we keep thinking we are a match for our pesky obsessions. We keep thinking that if we just try a little harder, or we make a vow to stop and really mean it this time, or we beat ourselves up a little bit more, then we will be rid of the enemies that heckle us. When will we learn to turn completely to God and invite his power to be released in us?

S.O.S.

As I wrestled with my compulsive attachment to the affection of young men, I made many attempts to stop the behavior. That usually lasted until the next attractive option came along. Life felt as though it was on a downward spiral, the waters were rising around my neck, and I knew I was out of control. In my desperation one evening, alone in my room, I cried out to God.

This time my cry was different. It wasn't just "God help me out of this fix; help me stop giving in to this temptation." Instead, my cry was one of profound longing. I knew nothing of Satan or spiritual battle, but the first thing I said was, "Satan, get out of here." That was followed by an honest, heartfelt confession: "God, I want you more than anything else in life." I wasn't concerned any longer about the sin that controlled me. I was pierced by a desperate longing to know and have and experience God in my life.

That event was pivotal. And what followed was supernatural.

It was so personal and mysterious that I am reticent to explain. I experienced something of God that I have never totally understood or experienced since. It was as though I was a battlefield, and that evening God did battle for me and conquered this enemy of my soul. He reached down, got his hands dirty, and delivered me from the swirling flood waters. He delivered me from the enemy that had held claim to me as its victim.

My fixation was no longer on trying to stop what I was doing. My fixation was on turning toward God with all my being and receiving him. What happened that evening for me was a spiritual encounter with God that broke the power that sin had held over my life. My body was set free, the chains broken and the power expelled.

I am not claiming that my experience is how it should be for everyone. There isn't a magic formula for God to work his power. Sometimes it happens in a decisive moment, and other times it is through a process. This is the point: God has power to deliver us. And his power is released when we desperately call to him from our deep place of longing.

The Reality of Temptation

I am not suggesting that what God did that evening conquered the temptation to sin once and for all or that God did everything from there on out and I did nothing. I had to continue to fight the good fight. I had to wait on God to fill the ache. I had to "live lonely" for a while. But for the first time I had the power to do it: to say no. My will had been freed from bondage.

Life Skills

Offering Ourselves Grace

The life skills we develop as we journey through the deep waters have to do with how we respond to our compulsive attachments. Most of the time when we first admit that there is something controlling us, our reaction is to try to stop the behavior, thought pattern, or coping mechanism. One of the ways we do that is to shame ourselves for choosing an unhealthy substitute. Shame is a way of relating to ourselves that says, "If I can get myself to feel bad enough about this, then I will want to be good!" It is not an effective strategy.

- Learn to suspend your reaction to reform yourself, especially the mechanism of shame.
- Instead, respond with grace toward your own humanity.
- As David Benner suggests, learn to respond to your attachments with *hospitality* rather than *hostility*, because you recognize them as a means of insight into your deeper longings for God.
- Ask God to show you what it is that you long for and how he wants to satisfy that longing.

Calling Out to God from Our Deepest Longings

Something powerful happens to us when we cease shaming or trying to reform ourselves and begin to call out to God from our true, pure, deep longings for him. Gerald May explains that when we start to live out of those deep longings:

> Energies that once were dedicated simply to relieving ourselves from pain now become dedicated to a larger goodness, more aligned with the true treasure of our hearts. Where we were once interested only in conquering a specific addiction, we are now claiming a deeper longing, and we are concerned with becoming more free from attachments in general, for the sake of love. (*Addiction and Grace*, p. 150)

- Stop expending all your energy on relieving your pain or conquering your addictive behavior.
- Instead, ask God to help you discover a "larger goodness" that is aligned with the true longings of your heart.
- Give in to that deeper longing to experience the love of God and to live a life of love; surrender your life to love.

Sitting with the Emptiness of Our Unmet Longings

In the landscape of the deep waters, we learn to call out to God from our most heartfelt longings. But we also learn to wait on God to fill us, rather than fill ourselves through whatever we can dish up. David cried out in Psalm 40:1, "I waited patiently for the LORD; / he turned to me and heard my cry." David knew the discipline of waiting in the emptiness of unmet longing. He waited, feeling the longing to be rescued and have something firm beneath his feet. He waited until God lifted him from the deep waters and met his heart's desire.

- When you feel the ache of longing, still the impulse to satisfy that need yourself.
- Sit with the emptiness and feel the hole while you embrace the hunger.
- Wait for God to fill the need in whatever way he chooses.

Everything That Isn't Us

As we spend time in the whirlpool of deep waters, it can begin to act as a centrifuge. The spinning separates who we are from all the things that we use to keep our false selves alive. The process is dizzying, but the end result can produce a more genuine wholeness as we separate from everything that isn't us.

Michelangelo took a similar approach as he fashioned his exquisite sculpture *David*. Someone admiring his work asked how he formed such an amazingly lifelike statue of David that seemed to capture his essence. Michelangelo's response was something like this: "I just chiseled away everything that wasn't David."

The deep waters, like erosion over the stones in a stream, begin to chisel away everything that isn't us. That is the transformational potential of our journey through the landscape of deep waters.

For Reflection and Conversation

- As you look back on your past journey, when have you spent time in the landscape of deep waters? Describe that time.

- What did you discover about yourself through this time of confronting a compulsive attachment? What did you discover about God?

- As you take stock of your life, what unhealthy attachments are you most troubled by right now? What is your typical way of dealing with them?

- In what ways do you struggle with shame? Describe them.

- How might you grow more in the act of offering yourself grace?

- What keeps you from turning fully to God and trusting his power to deliver you from the deep waters? How might you trust and rely on God more?

Chapter Eight

THE LAND BETWEEN

Luke 24:1-35

Entering the Chrysalis

O NE BLUSTERY WINTER DAY, SUE MONK KIDD HEADED
out on a walk to clear her head. For some time now, she had
been brooding in an awkward state betwixt and between, out
of sorts within herself and desperate to find relief. As she wandered, she stumbled upon an epiphany, a gift that spoke to
her about her travail and shed light on her dim passage of
uncertainty.

> I burrowed into the wind, my head down. I happened to look
> up again as I passed beneath the branches of a dogwood tree,
> and my eyes fell upon a curious little appendage suspended
> from a twig just over my head.
>
> I kept walking. *No, stop . . . look closer.* Not knowing what else
> to do but obey the inner impulse, I backed up and looked
> again. . . . *I had come upon a cocoon.*
>
> I was caught suddenly by a sweep of reverence, by a sensa-
> tion that made me want to sink to my knees. For somehow I
> knew that I had stumbled upon an epiphany, a strange gracing
> of my darkness. . . . In that moment God seemed to speak to me
> about transformation. About the descent and emergence of the
> soul. About hope. . . .

That was the moment the knowledge descended into my heart and I understood. *Really* understood. Crisis, change, all the myriad upheavals that blister the spirit and leave us groping— they aren't voices simply of pain but also of creativity. And if we would only listen, we might hear such times beckoning us to a season of waiting, to the place of fertile emptiness.

I turned . . . quickened by the moment. I knew. Dear God, I knew. I must enter the chrysalis. (*When the Heart Waits*, pp. 12-13)

The land between, as Sue Monk Kidd discovered, is an invitation to enter the chrysalis, to move into a place of mystery and wait for our rebirth. It is a time of transition between landscapes, a period of gestation as the budding of life takes shape and form and then moves us out from our cramped quarters to the landscape of what is to come. There is something about this landscape that can feel like emptiness. But if we are willing to live in it, we will begin to recognize it as a fertile loam of creativity where our soul descends and then emerges with a new, graceful identity.

The Land Between

The land between is the route of transition we take as we pass from one landscape to the next. We look behind us and can see where we have been. We look ahead but don't know exactly where we are going. We are somewhere in the middle, between "what was" and "what will be."

It's that breathtaking moment when the man on the flying trapeze lets go and is suspended in midair until the next trapeze meets his grip. In this liminal space, we find ourselves hanging in the middle of change, hoping the next trapeze will come and transport us safely to the other side.

There is ambiguity during this time, because we are transitioning from where we have been into an unknown, yet-to-be-determined future. The next landscape of life is ill-defined and uncertain.

Sometimes the land between feels exciting. There is a sense of adventure as the future unfolds, an anticipation of opportunities, possibilities, and growth. But at other times there is a feeling of grief in the air because a season of life is ending, the pages are turning to a new chapter, and the one we've been living is over.

If you are leaving the landscape of the desert, more than likely you will feel some relief and excitement that the grass may be greener on the other side of the land between. But if you have been in the promised land, it is certain that you will feel a loss as you depart such a rich and flourishing time of life to enter the womb of change.

Three Stages of Transition

In William Bridges's bestselling book *Transition: Making Sense of Life's Changes*, he defines three stages of transition: an ending, a neutral zone, and a beginning. When you enter the land between, you do so because something in your life is coming to an end. Usually that implies loss. It's possible that the loss is one we welcome. But often we feel sentimental about the ending, realizing that we can never repeat this time of life again.

Motherhood provides ample illustrations of those melancholy endings, when you are saying goodbye to an era while saying hello to a new one. It is common to feel a bittersweet ambivalence as you miss certain aspects of one stage while welcoming the new growth and increased freedom of the next.

As we enter the land between we are ending something, and that ending initiates entrance into a "neutral zone." *Neutral* may be a misnomer, because we often don't feel neutral about this in-between place. It can feel so ambiguous, unstable, and temporary that we find the experience disconcerting.

At some point, there is an awareness of beginning a new phase of life. Something has begun that opens up new possibilities and potential. It's as if you were in a subterranean tunnel and finally have emerged onto a superhighway with a number of exit ramps and new destinations to explore.

Transition is never seamless, and it is often difficult to differentiate where we are in the process. More easy to recognize is the inner turbulence that change incites: an awareness that the scenery of our lives is morphing, the climate we are entering is uncertain, and we had better prepare ourselves for whatever lies ahead.

Venues of Change

As individuals, we will move through a series of transitions over our lifetime. We are ending or beginning something virtually all the time. To further complicate things, we are living in a culture that is constantly changing. It's no wonder our heads are spinning.

One way we can enter the land between is when we enter a new life stage. Puberty might be one of the most identifiable and precarious new life stages, for both the person going through it and the parent trying to manage the volatility.

My unscientific analysis has shown that, for young girls, the onset of puberty is signaled when, while standing at the bathroom mirror, they throw their brush down in disgust, scream "I hate my hair!" run to their bedroom, and slam the door. I have witnessed this phenomenon three times, each when one of my girls was twelve or thirteen years old.

Certainly as groundbreaking and turbulent are the transitions into young adulthood and independence; midlife with all its potential and crisis; and retirement, the era of slowing down and aging. Each transition embodies the challenge of adjusting to the ending of an era while entering the nebulous in-between, as the person moves forward and embraces a new stage of life.

A second way we can enter the land between is when we take on a new role. During that time, we can expect that there will be an interval called the "adjustment period." Getting married, becoming a parent, going back to school, or beginning a new job will require a period of adapting to change.

Even more difficult are the roles we transition into because of significant loss, such as becoming a widow, a single parent, or single again after a divorce. Some adjustments to new roles come more easily, while others demand more work and some finesse.

A third way we can enter the land between is when we leave one community and enter a new one. Moving can be a tumultuous affair, as families are uprooted and transplanted. There is an in-between time when everyone is trying to find where they belong. Unfortunately this process usually takes longer than we expect, as we seek to reestablish our roots and sense of belonging.

My husband and I have a dear friend who left our community recently to begin a new role as a graduate student. He has been in transition, having been part of a tight-knit group of friends in a familiar city and now living in a new location with mostly new acquaintances. The flux of this in-between time has been hard on him. It has wrung a lot of life from him as he navigates through this middle ground.

Each of these transitions—a new life stage, a new role, or a new community—is brought on by physical or external factors. There is another kind of impetus into the land between that is instigated by the yearnings of our soul. This transition is what Sue Monk Kidd described in the excerpt from her book, *When the Heart Waits*. It illustrates a time of life when our soul is asking a new question.

She describes her musings in this way:

> During the days after my February walk, I asked myself what would happen if I could learn the spiritual art of cocooning. Might I discover a stilling of the soul that invites God and a new re-creation of life? Would I see that waiting, with all its quiet passion and hidden fire, is the real crucible of spiritual transformation? Would the posture of the cocoon allow me a way to shed old, embedded patterns of living and move into a more genuine humanity where the authentic self breaks through? (p. 14)

Sometimes growing pains in our soul lead us from where we have been to where we need to go to become more whole. New questions of a curious sort draw us toward growth and conversion. This journey can be filled with raucous storms and turbulent upheaval. However, when we wait it out in the storm—in the chrysalis—we are often transformed. That's where we shed the old stuff of our lives and become more the person God created us to be.

Consider Paul's description of this shedding in Ephesians 4:22-24: "You were taught, with regard to your former way of life, to put off your old self, which is being corrupted by its deceitful desires; to be made new in the attitude of your minds; and to put on the new self, created to be like God in true righteousness and holiness."

It is the nature of life to be ever-changing, vacillating between beginning and ending at some level all the time. As a result, we will often find ourselves in the land between. Sometimes our journey will last a short time, maybe a few weeks or months. But there are other times when we might feel that we are in transition for several years.

Times of Transition in the Biblical Story: Two on the Emmaus Road

Scanning the Bible, we see lots of in-between points. When God called Sarah and Abraham to leave their homeland and go toward his land of promise, they journeyed for some time in a land between. Then there was Israel's descent into the desert before returning to the promised land. One of the marked in-between periods is the four hundred years of peculiar silence between the Old and New Testaments.

The example I want to consider involves the transitional period after Christ's death and before his return to heaven. This brief period of forty or so days in the lives of Christ's followers was a disorienting time, as they dealt with all that had happened and tried to figure out how to move forward as his disciples.

During the beginning of that difficult time, a story is told of two followers of Christ who were traveling on a road toward Emmaus, sorting through the troubling, confusing events of Christ's arrest, crucifixion, death, and burial. Only one of the gospel writers, Luke, includes this story, though Mark mentions the occasion.

To put the story in context, it took place after Jesus' resurrection, when to our knowledge the only person he had appeared to was Mary Magdalene (John 20:10-18). These two disciples were not part of the band of twelve disciples, though they were obviously close to him (Luke 24:33). Only one of them is identified; his name is Cleopas. We don't really know who he is, though a woman who stood at the cross of Christ is referred to as the wife of Cleopas (John 19:25). So it's possible, though undeterminable, that this Cleopas is one and the same.

As the two disciples were walking along, "talking with each other about everything that had happened" (Luke 24:14), Jesus appeared and began walking alongside them, but they were kept from recognizing him. He asked them, "What are you discussing together as you walk along?" (Luke 24:17).

What We Discover About Ourselves in This Landscape

We Need to Process Change with Each Other

The first thing we notice in this narrative is that the two disciples took to the highway to process all the troubling events of the past few days. We don't know why they chose the road to Emmaus; perhaps it was home to one of them, or maybe a scenic route, or maybe just a good direction opposite all the turmoil and confusion in Jerusalem.

Whatever the reason, these two disciples were churning inside, trying to make sense of what had happened, where things had gone wrong, what they had missed. As if standing over the puzzle of life, they were trying to fit the pieces together. And so they headed off together to "talk and discuss these things."

When we enter the land between, we will need to find companions with whom we can process our experience. Because this landscape can be a disconcerting time, we will naturally feel upset and disoriented. And if we pay attention to our hearts, they will tell us that we need company and conversation to sort through the malaise.

Process, as a verb, means "to discuss the interpersonal dynamics and emotional content of an event or situation" (Encarta Dictionary, North America). And that's what we do when we process together. We work through and assimilate all that has happened in order to help us accept, understand, and move through what has happened.

This churning, resolving urge sometimes steams through us like a boiling teapot as we process all that is happening inside us and around us. Processing together is the therapy we need to glean as much as we can from the transformative landscape.

Unfortunately, we don't always choose to move toward each other. Because times of change can be tumultuous, they often don't bring out our best. Our equilibrium is thrown off and, as a result, we sometimes prefer to withdraw from company rather than move toward it. Undoubtedly, we will be better off if we can find, and be, reassuring companions on our own Emmaus roads.

One of the best books I have ever read is called *When God Interrupts: Finding New Life Through Unwanted Change* by M. Craig Barnes. In his book, Barnes describes the church as a "community of interrupted lives, where we come to confess our stories and search for God's purpose" (p. 42).

We are a community of people whose lives have been interrupted by change. We desperately need to come together and tell our stories and help one another find God in them. Offering spiritual direction involves discerning where God is involved in another's life. That is what we can offer one another as we process the transitions of life on the road to wherever.

We Struggle to Accept the Timing of Transitions

The second thing we learn about ourselves in the land between is our struggle with the time it takes to make transitions. Transition has an innate time frame, a speed (or lack of speed) at which it travels. Every transition we go through will require a certain pace in order to process and profit thoroughly from the time. What we discover in these transitions is a pull in one of two directions: we either delay transition by holding onto the past or try to speed up transition by moving on too quickly.

We Delay Transition by Holding Onto the Past

As the two disciples continued their journey to Emmaus, they described to the stranger (Jesus) everything that had happened.

> He asked them, "What are you discussing together as you walk along?"
> They stood still, their faces downcast. One of them, named Cleopas, asked him, "Are you only a visitor to Jerusalem and do not know the things that have happened there in these days?"
> "What things?" he asked.
> "About Jesus of Nazareth," they replied. "He was a prophet, powerful in word and deed before God and all the people. The chief priests and our rulers handed him over to be sentenced to death, and they crucified him; *but we had hoped that he was the one who was going to redeem Israel*" (Luke 24:17-21, emphasis added).

That final statement says a lot about the disciples' struggle in the land between, having experienced the death of their dreams. As the two friends processed what had happened, they acknowledged their sorrow that Jesus hadn't turned out to be who they had hoped. They pined away for the Jesus who was their delivering Messiah. They wanted to return to the past, to the way things were when this Messiah, who they had hoped would be a powerful political leader, would set the record straight and free Israel from its Roman oppression.

In the land between, we struggle to let go of what was or what we thought would be. We will feel the disappointment of our loss and know in our hearts that there is no turning back. It will never be the same.

Sometimes we can romanticize the past because it seems better to us than the no-man's land where we find ourselves.

Admittedly, we often prefer the known over the unknown, even if the known had its disadvantages. The Israelites, faced with the bleak and hazy terrain of the desert, longed to go back to Egypt even though they had been slaves there.

We Speed Up Transition by Moving On
Too Quickly

While we may struggle to let go of the past and delay the transition, we may also try to speed it up by moving on too quickly. The two disciples on the road to Emmaus seemed to have done that. It is curious that they didn't stay in Jerusalem with the other disciples, grieving and waiting patiently until they understood what they were to do.

These two weren't the only ones to move on too quickly. In John's Gospel we are told that even after Jesus had appeared to his disciples, Peter and several others returned to fishing (John 21). Their movements, like many of the actions we take in our own lives, are indicative of the impulse to speed up periods of ambiguity by moving on to something that is familiar or more concrete.

A case in point is how people grieve and handle transition in the death of a loved one. I just heard an interview of a family who lost their son in a plane crash over a year ago. The mother confessed in tears that she had not even touched her beloved son's room because she was unable to handle the grief of dismantling or removing anything that reminded her of her son. In contrast, I think of my own mother, who, less than two weeks after my father died, chose to clean out his closets and take everything in them to an urban mission.

As we journey through the land between, we are swept up in a current of transition that flows at a certain speed. Each transition has its own intrinsic timetable. Our challenge is to set aside our aversion to process and resist the impulse to manipulate the time that transition takes.

In the Land Between, God's Presence Often Seems Veiled

Another lesson we can draw from the Emmaus story is our diminished ability to recognize God's presence in the land between.

During their interchange with Jesus, the two disciples, for some undisclosed reason, were not able to recognize him. It is not clear if God prevented it; if Jesus looked so different they didn't recognize him; or if they were so distraught they simply didn't realize it was Jesus.

Whatever the cause of their temporary blindness, the two disciples were clueless that the man accompanying them along the road to Emmaus was the very man whose loss they were grieving.

Not only did they not recognize Jesus from his appearance; he later scolded them because they hadn't recognized him through the testimony of the prophets either. "'How foolish you are, and how slow of heart to believe all that the prophets have spoken! Did not the Christ have to suffer these things and then enter his glory?' And beginning with Moses and all the Prophets, he explained to them what was said in all the Scriptures concerning himself" (Luke 24:25-27).

When we travel through tenuous, unformed, vague times of our life, our vision of Jesus is often obscured by the haze. We can't see him in the landscape; we can't see him in his word. We are confused and anxious, groping through the fog that lingers over the land between.

What We Discover About God in This Landscape

Jesus Is Our Companion in Ordinary Life

When I consider a story like the Emmaus narrative, I often look for patterns in which Christ works in our lives and interacts with us. By patterns, I don't mean formulas or equations. I am looking for examples, samples, or precedents for how he appears in people's lives in the biblical story.

I find it curious and encouraging, for example, that Jesus chose to appear and walk alongside two obscure individuals who were in the thick of conversation talking about him. Later, when they were close to the village, they invited Jesus to stay with them, and they shared a meal together. There is something so familiar, so common, about the way Jesus joined them along their way.

Most of the story centers on the activities of ordinary life: walking, talking, eating, and resting. And Jesus is in the center of them all. This reminds us of Jesus' desire to walk with us on our journey and be present at our meals, in our conversations, and when we pause to rest. He wants to be our companion in the ordinary as we travel along our way.

There Is a Bigger Story and Jesus Has the Leading Role

As Jesus walked with the two disciples, he asked them questions and explained to them, "beginning with Moses and all the Prophets,... what was said in all the Scriptures concerning himself" (Luke 24:27).

What was it that Jesus was so adamant they understand? What was the point of his sermon? Of all the things he could have talked about, he was passionate to help these lost souls discover him in the bigger story of God.

He wanted them to know that the events of the preceding days were not a botched attempt by Jesus at saving the nation of Israel from the grip of Roman oppression; those events were in concert with God's purposes to offer a suffering savior for the redemption of the world.

Jesus wanted the disciples to see him in the words of the prophets—that he was the Christ, the lamb of God, sent to suffer for the sins of the world. He wanted to connect the dots for them, to reveal the steadfastness of God's redeeming purposes streaming throughout history. And he wanted them to know that he had the leading role in the drama.

When we are in the land between, we can feel as though God has no purpose and Jesus is hard to find. In this liminal space, life appears to lack substance, and it seems we are not operating according to *any* plan. Jesus wants us to know that a bigger story always exists. God is always involved, working redemptively in the midst of life's landscape. Even when we have suffered harm, misfortune, or mistakes in our smaller stories, he is working in them, through them, and in spite of them. As a result, we can take comfort because we are tethered to a bigger story of God's redeeming love, a story of which Jesus is *still* the central character.

Today, as history unfolds, God's purposes are still being accomplished through Jesus Christ. I am bolstered by the words of Psalm 33:10-11:

> The LORD foils the plans of the nations;
>   he thwarts the purposes of the peoples.
> But the plans of the LORD stand firm forever,
>   the purposes of his heart through all
>   generations.

Life Skills

Finding our way through the fog of the land between can be challenging. This terrain doesn't give us many cues about where we are and how much longer it will be until we get to the other side. In order to traverse the land between, we need to learn some life skills that will help us stay in the chrysalis and avoid a premature departure.

Looking in the Rearview Mirror to Understand Our Past

The first life skill we can learn is to look in the rearview mirror in order to understand our past. Jesus connected the dots for the two disciples on the road to Emmaus. It is important to allow him to do the same for us. One of the best vantage points we can have in order to understand our journey with God comes from looking in the rearview mirror.

• Take time to study where you have come from, in order to identify important life themes and discern God's movement in ways you had not seen.

• Journal your thoughts and make note of your findings so that you can identify God at work in the present and participate with him in his purposes.

Waiting in the Fog for Our Future to Take Shape

The second life skill we have the opportunity to learn is the art of waiting. We find it so hard to wait. We would rather be moving somewhere than waiting nowhere! Learning to wait is an art. It isn't, as some might surmise, a passive activity, twiddling our thumbs. Waiting is an active exercise.

• Learn the art of waiting by acknowledging and accepting that the point of the land between is for transformation, not simply to "get through it" so that you can move on to the next phase of life.

• Learn to slow down and pause before you act. Ask yourself if you are hanging onto the past or hurrying on to the future.

• As you wait, actively rest in God, allowing the season of waiting to "age" your soul.

Processing Our Stories with One Another and Searching for God's Purposes

The third life skill we learn is to process our stories with one another in order to discover the presence and purposes of God. The two disciples took to the road, which was a great place to walk and talk and process the stories of their lives. We need to do the same. This purposeful storytelling is a strong adhesive, bonding our communities together. When we learn one another's stories, we develop a history with one another.

• Seek out other companions with whom you feel comfortable and safe sharing your own personal journey with God in the land between.

- Be purposeful in sharing your story with those companions and ask for their insight.
- Listen to their stories, learn their history, and help them discover the purposes of God in the midst of their lives.

Using Our Spiritual Intuition to See the Bigger Story of God

Finally, in the land between, the fourth life skill we learn is to use our spiritual intuition to discern the bigger story of God. God, through his spirit, gives us the ability to recognize where he is involved in the world around us. But that ability requires spiritual intuition—the ability to see God's story weaving through our story, especially if we feel lost or in a fog in the land between. Here are some suggestions of how to develop your spiritual intuition:

- Pay attention to unusual experiences such as dreams or visions; when you read or listen to others, pay attention to words or phrases that stand out to you and linger in your mind; ask God to speak to you through those words.
- Notice recurring themes, events, or encounters and ask God for their meaning.
- Be receptive to God speaking through supposedly "non-sacred" elements such as art, movies, nature, and music. In your dialogue with God, listen with spiritual intuition for him to speak and help you see his story as it unfolds around you.

Free but Unable to Fly

Our journey through the land between is an invitation to enter the chrysalis. As we do, we may feel a strong urge to wriggle out, resisting the dark and cramped chamber. Consider the following parable, based on "Dryness and Dark Night" by

Gerald Heard, as a reminder of what happens if we prematurely escape our cocoon of transformation.

There once was a scientist who had devoted his life to developing a species of butterfly that would be the most beautiful the world had ever seen. After years of experimentation, he was certain that he had a chrysalis that would produce his genetic masterpiece.

On the day the butterfly was expected to emerge, the entire staff gathered around, champagne in hand, for the momentous birth. They watched breathlessly as the stunning creature began to break through the walls of its chrysalis.

First its right wing, then its body, then its left wing began to work its way out. The scientist and staff watched with eagerness. But the longer they watched, the more apparent it became that the butterfly was in trouble; its left wing was stuck to the mouth of the chrysalis.

The butterfly labored, growing more and more exhausted, until the scientist couldn't stand it any longer. He used a small scalpel and carefully cut the creature free. The staff cheered as the butterfly burst through the chrysalis and landed on the laboratory table.

Then silence fell over the room. The butterfly was free . . . but it could not fly (Christopher Isherwood, *Vedanta for the Western World*, p. 81).

If you are being called to enter the chrysalis, to travel through the land between, your greatest trial will be to remain long enough in this place of fertile emptiness so that when you emerge, you will not simply be free . . . you will be able to fly.

For Reflection and Conversation

• When have you spent time in the land between? What was that like for you?

• In what way is God inviting you to enter the chrysalis in your life right now?

• During transition, are you more inclined to hang onto the past or move things along too quickly? Explain what you mean.

• Who are the companions with whom you process your journey? How could you be more intentional in developing more meaningful spiritual companionship?

• Where in your life does God seem veiled? Are there any hints about the bigger story of God that are beneath the surface story of your life?

• Using your spiritual intuition, what do you notice in your life that might be a clue for you to discover God's bigger story?

CONCLUSION

Our Peregrine Journey

OUR JOURNEY WITH GOD THROUGH THE VARIED landscapes of life is reminiscent of the tradition of the Celtic Christian wanderers, called *peregrini*. These were individuals who began a pilgrimage by water, often in a small, oarless craft, on a journey led along by whatever current propelled them.

A story from the ninth century illustrates. Three Irishmen set sail in a small craft called a coracle, dispensing with its oars and floating across the sea to England. When they arrived on shore in Cornwall, they were escorted to the court of King Alfred. Asked by the king where they were headed, the men replied that they "stole away because we wanted for the love of God to be on pilgrimage, we cared not where" (Esther de Waal, *The Celtic Way of Prayer*, p. 2).

The heart of the peregrine journey is a sense of purposeful wandering through life, open to its generous topography, believing that in it one will discover a bigger God and a bigger life. To peregrinate means to wander about in the wide open spaces. It is not an aimless wandering but a purposeful one. Yet the purpose is not a prescribed destination but a pilgrimage of discovery.

Through our peregrine journey, we are consenting to be led along by a larger and more mysterious current that becomes our providence. Carried along by the unfolding currents of God's story and our own, we find ourself living a bigger, fuller life than if we had simply remained in a safe and familiar landscape.

Our search is not simply to find God. Nor is it to find ourselves. Rather, it is to be present to God and ourselves through the varied landscapes of life.

APPENDIX

How to Host a *Wide Open Spaces of God* Event

IF YOU ARE INTERESTED IN HOSTING A *WIDE OPEN Spaces of God* retreat, conference, or course, it would be my pleasure to come and speak for your event. Please contact me through my website at www.wideopenspacesofgod.org.

You may also provide your own presenters and use the material in this book in a variety of venues. The following suggestions will help in organizing and implementing your *Wide Open Spaces of God* event.

I recommend that you form a team of six to twelve people, depending on the size of your event. Each area of responsibility works best with at least two individuals sharing the tasks. The following are job descriptions that define the areas of responsibility and their tasks.

Team Leader

Job Description

Job Focus: To provide leadership in the planning and implementation of a *Wide Open Spaces of God* event; to delegate responsibilities to the subteams described below and provide oversight in the execution of their responsibilities.

Responsibilities

- Invite between six and twelve individuals to serve on the team. (Choose individuals with whom it would be a pleasure to work and for whom you have confidence in their character, chemistry, and competence.)
- Convene between six and nine months in advance of the event. Decide together on the date, time frame, and location and what type of event you will hold: a retreat (day or overnight), a conference, or a course over several weeks.
- Establish your meeting schedule and dates from the first meeting until the celebration after the event.
- Meet monthly until six weeks prior to the event. Then meet biweekly until the event.
- Delegate responsibility and authority to each subteam; designate a point person for each subteam to lead that team and communicate with you; go over the job focus and responsibilities with each subteam, clarifying any questions.
- Maintain regular communication with your team, especially with each subteam point person.
- Prepare the agenda for each meeting and e-mail a meeting summary after each meeting.
- Take time during each meeting to strengthen the relational connection among the team members; invite them to share their stories with one another.
- Provide vision and encouragement for the team; always remind them of the *why* of what they are doing.
- Arrive early to the event and offer support to your team in whatever way is needed.
- Lead your team in prayer throughout the planning process.
- Plan a celebration for your team to take place a week or two after the event. Celebrate together what God did in the lives of the attendees. Celebrate what you saw God bring out in each of your team members.

Publicity and Promotion

Job Description

Job Focus: To provide clear, effective, and appealing publicity and promotion of your event so that the maximum number of people are informed of the event and decide to attend. (You typically need to invite six times as many people as will attend your event.)

Responsibilities

- Contact me through my website (www.wideopenspaces ofgod.org) to receive the *Wide Open Spaces of God* template for a brochure or e-mail invitation for your event.
- Use the *Wide Open Spaces of God* template provided or design your own communications pieces (postcards, brochures, e-mail invitations, and posters) to promote your event.
- Post the date and title of your event on your website six to twelve months in advance.
- Send out a promotional teaser by e-mail and/or mail six months in advance, including the title of the event, date, time, location, and a very short description.
- Include complete event information and a downloadable brochure and registration form on your website six months prior to the event.
- Send out the brochure and/or e-mail invitation eight weeks prior to the registration deadline.
- Send out a "Registration Deadline" reminder e-mail two weeks before the deadline.
- Promote your event at strategic gatherings where you can inform groups of people at one time.
- Promote your event through widely read publications, on radio stations, and TV channels in your community.
- Remember that with all the technology available, personal invitation is still the very best promotion of all! Cast vision in your community to bring a friend.

Registration and Finance

Job Description

Job Focus: To provide multiple, easy, and accessible ways to register attendees; to oversee financial operations with the goal of making the event self-supporting (that is, the income from the attendees covers the cost of the event).

Responsibilities

- Registration should be made as easy and accessible as possible, with the option of registering by mail, online, or in person at your church or ministry location.
- If you do not have the ability to receive online payment, provide a downloadable registration form that can be mailed with a check.
- Determine a registration deadline based on facility and catering requirements. Make sure the deadline is clearly stated on the promotional materials.
- Determine the total cost of your event based on your fixed expenses, such as facility costs, speaker honorarium, decorations, equipment rental (audiovisual, tables, chairs, and so on), promotional and conference printed materials, refreshments and meals.
- Determine the number of participants you hope to attend based on available space and past experience. If this is your first event, consider that approximately one in six individuals who receive a *personal* invitation (that is, through e-mail, mail, or a friend) will attend.
- Divide the total cost of the fixed expenses by the number of projected attendees to determine what you will charge each individual. It is always best to be conservative on the number of attendees and generous on the cost of the event. However, make sure the cost per attendee is appropriate for your demographics and reasonable for the event.

- Set budget amounts for each subteam or area of responsibility: speaker honorarium, Publicity and Promotions, Environment (facility, equipment, decorations, and refreshments/meals), and Program (technical equipment and printed materials). Remind each subteam to save all receipts.
- Collect registrations and create a master spreadsheet with information on each attendee, including name, address, telephone number, e-mail, and type of payment (check, credit card, cash, scholarship, or no payment).
- Print name tags from the master list.
- Handle cancellations (returned checks).
- Collect and deposit checks.
- Pay vendors.
- Keep a record of all transactions and receipts.
- Set up a registration check-in table at the event and assign hosts who greet and register attendees.

Environment

Job Description

Job Focus: To create an attractive and inviting environment in your meeting space and provide satisfying refreshments so that each attendee feels comfortable and cared for.

Responsibilities

- It is important for attendees to feel that the meeting space is safe, inviting, and as intimate as possible. Avoid using a room that is too big for the number of participants you are hosting. Stay away from an open atrium where there might be a lot of traffic noise or distractions.
- Make sure the sanctuary, auditorium, chapel, or meeting room is able to be set at a comfortable temperature.
- Lighting is a key element. Make sure the presenters have

adequate lighting on them in order to be seen and the participants have enough lighting to take notes. Good lighting will create warmth and a receptive environment for interaction.

• Check with the Program subteam to ensure that the space accommodates the group's technical needs (such as screens, lighting, sound system, PowerPoint projection, DVD player).

• Create ambiance through special decorations (entry doors, stage area, and tables) that capture the *Wide Open Spaces of God* theme. (If I speak at your event, I will bring nine landscape posters for display.)

• Because the participants will be sitting for some length of time, it is important to have comfortable chairs. Round tables can be a good option for note-taking and interaction. If tables aren't available, having movable chairs can allow participants to turn together and form small circles.

• Determine if you need to rent additional tables and chairs to accommodate the number of attendees. Place the order at least two months in advance.

• Determine how many snack times and meals you want, based on the length of your event. These are helpful to create downtime, foster a relational environment, and help the attendees stay focused and have energy.

• Choose a menu that has broad appeal, providing options if possible. Determine if you will have the meals catered or will prepare them yourselves. A buffet-style setup is generally more economical and offers variety.

• Purchase all paper goods, snacks, food, and drinks needed.

• Set up the meeting space, drink and coffee stations, and buffet lines with good visibility and traffic flow.

• Schedule setup and tear-down times with the team. Recruit additional people for assistance, if necessary.

Program

Job Description

Job Focus: To design a meaningful and engaging program and flow for the event that balances content, contemplation, and interaction; to select and prepare all the artistic, technical, and programmatic elements; to smoothly implement all the elements of the program so that the event has maximum impact in the attendees' lives.

Responsibilities

- Determine how many landscapes and which ones you want to present during your event. This should be discussed with the entire team. (You can customize your event by choosing which landscapes address the most relevant needs of your community.)
- Determine who you want to ask to present which landscapes, then extend the invitations and confirm the responses. If you are interested in having me speak at your event, you may contact me through my website: www.wideopenspacesofgod.org.
- Designate a gifted master of ceremonies to moderate the event.
- Determine the order of the landscapes and the programmatic elements that you want to include. I am happy to help you with this process. For ideas, see the section below titled "Setting Up Each Landscape." (If I speak at your event, I will bring with me the creative elements that correspond with the landscapes you are offering.)
- If you want to have worship during the event, decide when and how long for each worship experience and invite a worship leader or worship band to lead the worship.
- Make sure you have a well-trained, competent sound technician to run all the technical elements. This is critical to the effectiveness of your event.

- Prepare all the materials for the sound technician, such as artistic elements, PowerPoint slides, and movie clips.
- Type up a copy of the flow of the event for each team member, as well as for all presenters, worship leaders, and the sound technician.
- Create and reproduce any materials and structured notes for the event.
- Purchase folders or notebooks for each attendee and assemble them with event information, a schedule, and structured notes. (I can provide structured notes upon request.)
- Arrive early to the event and set up the sound system; walk through the flow of the program with the MC, those involved in the program, and the sound technician; and run through all PowerPoint slides and movie clips to make sure they are running properly.
- Assign someone to be the timekeeper during the event, monitoring when things need to begin and end and cueing the MC and speakers.

Prayer

Job Description

Job Focus: To cover all elements of this event in prayer, listening to God for his plans and asking for his involvement in every detail; to pray for and with the presenters and worship leaders; to be present during the event to offer healing prayer for those who ask.

Responsibilities

- Invite as many people as possible to pray regularly for this event.
- Schedule a few specific times of prayer together as a team; use the time to sit and listen for God to unveil what he has on his heart to do.

- Create a list of prayer requests to circulate among those who will pray for this event.
- Ask each subteam, the speakers, and the worship leader or leaders for any ways you can support them in prayer.
- During the event, have individuals praying throughout the time and available to pray with anyone who needs prayer.
- If possible, have a prayer chapel where individuals can go for quiet prayer.
- Provide trained caregivers to offer healing prayer for those who would like for someone to pray with them.
- After the event, praise God for all that he did. Publish any specific ways that God worked, being careful not to name persons or share confidential information.

Setting Up Each Landscape

You can present up to nine different landscapes, including the wide open spaces themselves, which can be treated as a separate landscape. The nine landscapes fall into three categories:
- **Landscapes of sorrow**: the desert, the valley of darkness, the deep waters
- **Landscapes of challenge**: the mountain of God, the land of exile, the land between
- **Landscapes of beauty**: the promised land, the green pastures, the wide open spaces

Depending on how many landscapes you are interested in covering, I recommend that you consider at least one from each category. (I typically allow two hours for each landscape, which includes the presentation, some time of reflection, interaction with others, and the artistic elements.)

Many teams are reluctant to offer one of the landscapes of suffering, but my experience has been that these landscapes are powerful because they invite the attendees to become more vulnerable and honest about their lives. That is entirely your call. Pray for discernment as you select your landscapes.

The following are some suggestions of ways you can set up each landscape. (In a few cases I've provided more than one suggestion.) The way you set up the landscape is contingent on the size of your event. If you host a conference of hundreds, then the setup may not be conducive to large-group interaction. In that case, have the participants turn to the person or two next to them to discuss the prompt. Even in groups of several hundred, however, you can solicit responses from the large group if the presenter can move into the audience and repeat the responses so everyone hears. (This actually creates a more intimate environment and sense of unified experience.)

As mentioned earlier, if I speak at your event, I will bring all the artistic elements with me. When I present, I use an interactive style of teaching, stopping at certain points and asking a question and engaging responses. At the end of each landscape, I recommend a time of personal reflection or small group discussion. *You can use any or all of the questions at the end of each chapter for discussion.*

The Wide Open Spaces

Setup: Watch scene eight from the film *The Matrix*. (End the clip when Morpheus and Neo stand up to walk out of the room.) Discuss the question, *What does it mean, spiritually speaking, to "take the red pill or the blue pill"?* Talk about it in small groups of three or four and then solicit feedback in the large group.

The Desert

Setup 1: Show a photograph of a person who appears to have experienced loss. (I use a well-known photograph of a woman during the Great Depression.) Ask the question, *What do you notice about this person? What stands out to you? What do you suppose her story to be?* Discuss in small groups or as a large group.

Setup 2: Watch the scene from the movie *Forrest Gump* in which Lieutenant Dan is on the edge of his shrimp boat, yelling at God. Ask the question, *How do you respond to this scene? What do you think is happening to Lieutenant Dan?*

The Promised Land

Setup: Listen to a version of the song "Somewhere Over the Rainbow." (I use a recording by the late singer Eva Cassidy. It is incredible!) Ask the question, *What, in your opinion, is this song about?* Discuss in small groups. Share responses with the large group.

The Mountain of God

Setup 1: Listen to the song by Bebo Norman, "Walk Down This Mountain." Ask the question, *What does it mean to offer up this broken cup to find the meaning of it all?* Discuss in small groups. Share responses with the large group.

Setup 2: Place in the center of each table or small group a single article related to mountain climbing, such as a backpack, boot, water bottle, pickax, or set of ropes. Label each article and its use. Ask the small group to come up with a spiritual metaphor for each article. Discuss how the article might aid us on our climb up the mountain of God. Have one person from each small group share their group's response.

The Valley of Darkness

Setup 1: Have each participant who is willing put on a blindfold. Give the blindfolded participants some simple instructions, such as "Take three steps forward; turn a quarter turn to the left; walk backward two steps," and so on. After several commands, ask participants on the count of three to point to where they think their chair is and then take off the blindfold. Have them discuss what the experience was like.

Setup 2: Ask the question, *Do you ever remember being afraid of the dark?* Share that experience with your small group.

The Green Pastures

Setup: Project on PowerPoint slides a series of images corresponding with each image in the chapter: a shepherd leading his sheep to pasture; a shepherd going out after lost sheep; a shepherdess healing a wounded sheep. (If you search the Internet, there are a number of images in the public domain that you can use.) Engage the attendees with the question, *What stands out to you in this image; what do you notice?*

The Land of Exile

Setup: Watch the opening scene to the movie *The Upside of Anger.* (End when the funeral scene is over.) Ask the questions, *How have you seen anger change someone in your life? Have you ever seen an upside of anger?*

The Deep Waters

Setup: Use for discussion the six case studies shown below. Pass out one case study per small group. (Depending on your attendance, more than one small group can discuss each case study.) Ask the questions, *To what has this individual formed an unhealthy attachment? What need is this person trying to fill?* Discuss in the small groups.

Linda

Linda grew up never feeling like anybody took her seriously. As the baby of the family, she was often chided for her immaturity. Through childhood wounds, she had a deep-seated feeling of inferiority and insignificance. Perceiving herself as small and impotent, disadvantaged because of some innate helplessness, she grew to have resentment for her plight.

After going through a divorce and becoming a single parent, Linda began to notice that the only time she ever felt powerful was when she got angry. Anger helped her feel more in control or dominant and less intimidated or bullied, especially by her ex-husband. So Linda began to use anger to hide her feelings of vulnerability and inferiority. Whenever she felt threatened or felt that her life was out of control, she would express anger to reestablish herself or reinforce her boundaries.

But before long she felt powerless to stop her angry responses to life. One day she became furious with her teenage son for talking back to her. Her anger escalated out of control, and in a fit of rage she struck him across the face. At once she saw the pain she had inflicted on him. Overcome by shame, Linda realized the grip her anger now had on her life and her inability to control it.

Kevin

Kevin was a high-energy person. He was always moving, and usually fast. The one thing Kevin avoided at all costs was being alone. He hated it when all his buddies had something to do and he was left to fend for himself. Being by himself made him feel irritable and anxious. He dreaded being left alone with his own thoughts.

As long as Kevin stayed busy and connected to somebody, he felt better. If he was driving, he usually made business calls on his cell phone. If he was home alone in his apartment, he had to have the television on or some noise to fill up the quiet. He planned ahead for the weekend, making sure he had something to do, often taking on the role of social chairman for all his friends. If he had free time, he would hang out in a coffee shop just so he could avoid being still and quiet and away from people.

This incessant striving and avoiding stillness ate away at him. Before long, Kevin was frayed and exhausted. One weekend all of his friends were gone or busy, and he was forced to be by himself for an extended time. Pressing through the resistance, he sat and took stock of his life. He didn't really like the person he was becoming. He hated the agitation that was eating away his insides. Kevin finally faced the reality of his unhappiness with himself and the way he was living his life.

Christine

Christine was a romantic. She loved fairy tales, romance novels, and chick flicks. Something in them spoke to her heart's longing to be loved and lovely, a princess to some Prince Charming. Her marriage to Greg had become stale, the romance having faded. She felt sad and disappointed, wondering if she would ever feel pursued and lovely again.

One afternoon at her daughter's soccer game, she sat next to another parent, a father of one her daughter's teammates. They struck up a conversation, chatting about the game, their kids, and life. He was warm and charming and seemed genuinely interested in her. When the game was over they said good-bye, and as he left he gave her a wink.

That night as she lay next to her sleeping husband, this man came to her mind. His wink stirred something in her heart. She began to fantasize about what it would be like to be pursued by him; what he might say and what she might say in return. She pictured flirting with him and him flirting back. Christine noticed how it thrilled her heart to imagine feeling attractive to him. She liked the feeling and so she began to daydream about this fantasy romantic relationship.

Before long she couldn't get him out of her mind. Her fantasies became more and more intimate, to the point that they became sexual. Her heart felt alive with passion and excitement from this imaginary relationship but more and more dead to her own marriage. Christine felt concerned and guilty, trapped because she couldn't stop thinking about the other man and more estranged than ever from her own husband.

Eric

Eric was certain in his faith and deeply devoted to God. He had been raised by Christian parents and was grateful for his upbringing and the love and commitment his parents had toward Christ, which made their family so strong.

Eric worked very hard to grow in his faith. He followed a stringent Bible-reading schedule, attended church without fail, and served as an elder. On the way to work almost every day, he listened to a favorite Bible teacher. Beyond Eric's devotion to God, he was a loyal friend and tried to pray regularly for those in his circle of friends. On the days that he didn't practice these spiritual disciplines, Eric never felt quite right.

But unexpectedly, Eric began to feel a dark cloud of gloom lingering over him. It felt as if God had slipped into the shadows of life. He no longer felt God's comfort or a sense of his presence. Eric was alarmed and frustrated that he couldn't control the darkness through some spiritual discipline. He grasped feverishly for something that would lift his spirits and bring God closer. But nothing he did helped.

Eric began to experience depression from the loss of control he had over his spiritual life. Everything he had ever used to keep him close to God was failing him. Discouragement and disillusionment made it difficult to keep trying. Lost in this deep pit, feeling unacceptable to God, Eric was frozen with fear that God had abandoned him.

Rachel

Rachel wanted more than anything to be a good wife and mother. But having three kids in three years had overwhelmed and exhausted her. Her days felt long, monotonous, and boring as she cared for her little ones and waited listlessly for her husband to come home from work and relieve her.

Rachel craved time to herself, a little space to breathe. She felt increasingly as though she were losing the parts of her identity that defined her before she became a mother. As the afternoons dragged on, the only relief she found was in having a glass of wine while making dinner and waiting for her husband. It seemed to help take the edge off, so that she could survive the incessant cries, quarrels, and demands of her children.

But over time Rachel noticed that a single glass of wine wouldn't do it; she needed two or three to have the same effect. It scared her to see herself needing this kind of fix. But it seemed to be the only way to endure the long afternoon.

One day when things were especially stressful, she gave in and drank the entire bottle. A neighbor dropped by to borrow something, and Rachel couldn't conceal her intoxication. The neighbor seemed embarrassed and left quickly. Now Rachel's secret was out. Filled with shame, she paced anxiously, wondering who else would find out. She was powerless not only to stop drinking but also to keep her secret to herself.

Michael

Michael lived with an incessant drive for order. He valued it in his home and at work, striving fastidiously to keep everything in its place and his environment clean and neat. His wife and kids knew the rules: where to take off their shoes, place the mail, and hang their coats.

Michael's personal life was disciplined and focused as well. He exercised with regularity, kept himself fit, and always watched what he ate. He strove to do everything expected of him and everything he expected of himself. Most people admired him for his dependability and competence—that is, with the exception of his teenage daughter, Becca.

Becca was starting to act out. Complaining about all the rules and the structure that her dad placed over her life, she began to show resentment because of her lack of personal freedom. It wasn't fair that she could never hang out with her friends if her bedroom wasn't clean or her homework wasn't finished. It irritated her that her dad was so controlling and tried to force Becca to be the person he thought she should be.

One night Becca had had enough, and so she sneaked out after her parents were in bed. She met up with some friends, and they prowled around the neighborhood, looking for a prank to pull. Finding a neighbor's car unlocked, they slipped it into neutral and let it roll into the middle of the street. About that time a porch light came on at the neighbor's house. The neighbor saw them and recognized Becca.

Michael was awakened by a ringing phone and an angry neighbor on the other end. Horrified by his daughter's behavior and incredulous at how this could have happened, Michael lost control. His anger raged, and then he broke down. In the wake of his anger, Michael felt estranged from his family and even from himself. He couldn't do it anymore. He couldn't keep it all together. He couldn't make his life work this way.

The Land Between

Setup: Place a chrysalis in the center of each table, or project a picture of a chrysalis on PowerPoint. Have the participants either journal or discuss with two or three others, *What does it mean to me to "enter the chrysalis"?* Open the discussion to the large group.

My experience, having offered *The Wide Open Spaces of God* to hundreds of individuals and groups, has been overwhelmingly positive. Almost instantly the participants connect with the landscape metaphors and begin to use that language. It is apparent that they feel more capable of framing their own journey with God through the use of these metaphors. Participants come alive with excitement and hope as they discover more of God and more of themselves through the landscapes of their lives. Based on my own experience, I have every reason to believe that your workshop can have the same impact, and that you and your group will be blessed as I have been.

BIBLIOGRAPHY

Barnes, M. Craig. *When God Interrupts: Finding New Life Through Unwanted Change.* Downers Grove, Ill.: InterVarsity, 1996.

Benner, David G. *The Gift of Being Yourself: The Sacred Call to Self-Discovery.* Downers Grove, Ill.: InterVarsity, 2004.

Bridges, William. *Transitions: Making Sense of Life's Changes.* New York: Perseus Books, 1980.

Encarta Dictionary, North America. http://encarta.msn.com/.

Gire, Ken. *The North Face of God: Hope for the Times When God Seems Indifferent.* Wheaton, Ill.: Tyndale, 2005.

Isherwood, Christopher. *Vedanta for the Western World.* London: George Allen & Unwin, 1961.

Kidd, Sue Monk. *The Secret Life of Bees.* New York: Penguin, 2005.

———. *When the Heart Waits.* San Francisco: HarperSanFrancisco, 2006.

Mason, Mike. *The Gospel According to Job: An Honest Look at Pain and Doubt from the Life of One Who Lost Everything.* Wheaton, Ill.: Crossway Books, 1994.

May, Gerald. *Addiction and Grace: Love and Spirituality in the Healing of Addictions.* New York: Harper & Row, 1988.

National Institute of Mental Health. "The Numbers Count: Mental Illness in America." http://www.upliftprogram.com/depression_stats.html#statistics.

New Bible Commentary: Revised. 3rd ed., revised and reset. London: InterVarsity, 1970.

Newell, J. Philip. *Promptings from Paradise.* Mahwah, N.J.: Paulist Press, 2000.

Palmer, Parker. *Let Your Life Speak: Listening for the Voice of Vocation.* San Francisco: Jossey-Bass, 2000.

United Methodist Hymnal. Nashville: The United Methodist Publishing House, 1989.

The Upside of Anger. DVD. Directed by Mike Binder. Los Angeles: New Line Productions, 2005.

de Waal, Esther, *The Celtic Way of Prayer.* New York: Doubleday, 1997.